MW00618322

"Most of the women I know long for mothers and sisters who will walk with us, navigate challenges beside us, and offer us wisdom when we don't know which way is up. Luckily, Tiffany Bluhm and her coalition of powerhouse women have seen that longing and answered it with a round of introductions. As it turns out, the women we've been waiting for were around us—and within us—the whole time."

—**Shannon K. Evans**, author of *The Mystics Would Like a Word*, *Feminist Prayers for My Daughter*, and *Rewilding Motherhood*

"Our collective flourishing requires a practice of solidarity, which is embodied within the very structure of this book. Tiffany invites us to celebrate historical figures and biblical matriarchs who inspire us as we wrestle with God, surrounded by the wisdom of our sisters. Individuals and communities will feel empowered as they learn from this collection of voices."

—**Sandra María Van Opstal**, pastor, professor, and author of *The Next Worship*

"Immerse yourself in the stories, lives, and actions of biblical women and historical figures for healing, restoration, and flourishing. This devotional by Tiffany Bluhm is refreshing, nourishing, and empowering. Read and reflect on Bluhm's words for sustenance, self-care, and encouragement."

—**Grace Ji-Sun Kim**, professor, Earlham School of Religion; author of *When God Became White* and *Invisible*

"*The Women We've Been Waiting For* is a bold and beautiful reminder of all the women—in Scripture and beyond—who have gone before us. Through stories of those who exhibit both tender vulnerability and fierce strength, Bluhm and others invite us to ponder, to grieve, to celebrate, to hope, and to bring our full selves to the sacred table for the sake of our individual and collective flourishing."

—**Kat Armas**, author of *Abuelita Faith* and host of *The Protagonistas* podcast

Previous Books by Tiffany Bluhm

Prey Tell:
Why We Silence Women Who Tell the Truth
and How Everyone Can Speak Up

She Dreams:
Live the Life You Were Created For

Never Alone:
Exchanging Your Tender Hurts for God's Healing Grace

THE WOMEN WE'VE BEEN WAITING FOR

A 40-DAY DEVOTIONAL FOR SELF-CARE, RESILIENCE, AND COMMUNAL FLOURISHING

TIFFANY BLUHM

Brazos Press

a division of Baker Publishing Group
Grand Rapids, Michigan

© 2024 by Tiffany Bluhm

Published by Brazos Press
a division of Baker Publishing Group
Grand Rapids, Michigan
BrazosPress.com

Printed in the United States of America

All rights reserved. No part of this publication may be reproduced, stored in a retrieval system, or transmitted in any form or by any means—for example, electronic, photocopy, recording—without the prior written permission of the publisher. The only exception is brief quotations in printed reviews.

Library of Congress Cataloging-in-Publication Data
Names: Bluhm, Tiffany, author.
Title: The women we've been waiting for : a 40-day devotional for self-care, resilience, and communal flourishing / Tiffany Bluhm.
Description: Grand Rapids, Michigan : Brazos Press, a division of Baker Publishing Group, [2024] | Includes bibliographical references.
Identifiers: LCCN 2024008560 | ISBN 9781587436390 (cloth) | ISBN 9781493447886 (ebook)
Subjects: LCSH: Women in the Bible. | Bible—Devotional literature. | Christian women.
Classification: LCC BS575 .B577 2024 | DDC 242/.643—dc23/eng/20240430
LC record available at https://lccn.loc.gov/2024008560

Unless otherwise indicated, Scripture quotations are from the Holy Bible, New International Version®, NIV®. Copyright © 1973, 1978, 1984, 2011 by Biblica, Inc.® Used by permission of Zondervan. All rights reserved worldwide. www.zondervan.com. The "NIV" and "New International Version" are trademarks registered in the United States Patent and Trademark Office by Biblica, Inc.®

Scripture quotations labeled CEB are from the Common English Bible. © Copyright 2011 by the Common English Bible. All rights reserved. Used by permission.

Scripture quotations labeled CSB are from the Christian Standard Bible. Copyright © 2017 by Holman Bible Publishers. Used by permission. Christian Standard Bible® and CSB® are federally registered trademarks of Holman Bible Publishers, all rights reserved.

Scripture quotations labeled ESV are from The Holy Bible, English Standard Version® (ESV®), copyright © 2001 by Crossway, a publishing ministry of Good News Publishers. Used by permission. All rights reserved. ESV Text Edition: 2016

Scripture quotations labeled GNT are from the Good News Translation in Today's English Version-Second Edition. Copyright © 1992 by American Bible Society. Used by permission.

Scripture quotations labeled Message are from The Message, copyright © 1993, 2002, 2018 by Eugene H. Peterson. Used by permission of NavPress. All rights reserved. Represented by Tyndale House Publishers.

Scripture quotations labeled NASB are from the (NASB®) New American Standard Bible®, Copyright © 1960, 1971, 1977, 1995, 2020 by The Lockman Foundation. Used by permission. All rights reserved. www.lockman.org

Scripture quotations labeled NET are from the NET Bible® copyright ©1996, 2019 by Biblical Studies Press, L.L.C. http://netbible.com. All rights reserved.

Scripture quotations labeled NLT are from the Holy Bible, New Living Translation, copyright © 1996, 2004, 2015 by Tyndale House Foundation. Used by permission of Tyndale House Publishers, Carol Stream, Illinois 60188. All rights reserved.

Scripture quotations labeled WEB are from the World English Bible.

Cover design by Dominique Jones

Published in association with Joy Eggerichs Reed of Punchline Agency.

Baker Publishing Group publications use paper produced from sustainable forestry practices and postconsumer waste whenever possible.

24   25   26   27   28   29   30   7   6   5   4   3   2   1

To the women who have gone before us,
the ones who have dismantled systems that made
no room for our flourishing:

may we glean from your lives well lived

Contents

Preface

In this devotional, I intertwine formation practices and stories of renewal. As you read, I ask you to consider how our flourishing is the result of a lifelong walk with the God of Mary and Hagar, Deborah and Esther, Naomi and Elizabeth. Scripture, stories, insights, prayers, and questions to ponder are tucked into each entry of *The Women We've Been Waiting For* in hopes of encouraging you to lean on the Divine as you seek refreshment for yourself and for others.

The women who contributed to this devotional are treasured voices I listen to: women who have challenged me to think differently about the Creator. These are formidable women whose unique expressions of the gospel have beckoned me to live a beautiful story without bending to the demands of grind culture or the will of whiteness. They are my sisters, women of integrity who spend their lives inviting others to take their place at the table while pursuing the upside-down kingdom.

I pray that as you immerse yourself in the stories of the women in this devotional you'll be transformed, challenged, and convicted by the Divine. I pray that you will gain insight into yourself in their rage, their frustration, their losses, their audacity, their hopes, their desires, and their victories. They wanted what we all long for: renewal and refreshment. May their longing be our reality as we faithfully pursue repentance, solidarity, formation, and liberation.

Contributors

Ariana Altiery-Rivera is a Chicago-raised Latina, non-profit professional, and founder of the online community @latinaslovingjesus. She is a leader at World Vision, which is a humanitarian aid organization that partners with churches in the United States to lift communities all over the world out of poverty. Her work focuses on strategies of cultural competency and pastoral care. In addition, Ariana coaches women who lead ministries and travels to church conferences where she trains leaders.

Lucretia Carter Berry is the visionary founder of Brownicity.com, whose mission is to foster education designed to inspire a culture of justice and belonging for all. Her research and experience intersect curriculum and instruction and multicultural education. A wife in an interracial marriage and mom of three multi-ethnic children, she brings personal and professional experience to serve the public sector with her books, *Hues of You: An Activity Book for Learning about the Skin You Are In* (2022), *What LIES Between Us: Fostering First Steps toward Racial Healing* (2016), *Teaching for Justice and Belonging: A Journey for Educators and*

Parents (2022); TED Talks; courses; and coaching that quell fears and inspire hope.

Kayla Craig, a former journalist, combines curiosity and compassion in her writing. She is the author of *Every Season Sacred* and *To Light Their Way* and founded the popular Liturgies for Parents Instagram account, weekly podcast, and newsletter. Kayla lives in Iowa with her husband and four children.

Ashlee Eiland is a thought leader, writer, and Bible teacher who exists to join in God's redemptive work here on earth. Her work has one purpose: to help humanity build bridges back to the truth of who God is and between one another in whole and healing relationships. Ashlee formerly served as a lead co-pastor at Mars Hill Bible Church in West Michigan. She and her husband live in Grand Rapids with their three kids.

Susie Gamez is Canadian by birth, Korean by heritage, Mexican by marriage, and American by immigration. She longs to make the reconciling love of Jesus come alive through Scripture and is known for speaking on God's love for those on the margins, God's heart for justice, and the joys and complexities of cross-cultural dynamics. Susie and her husband, Marcos, met at Fuller Theological Seminary while getting their master's degrees in intercultural studies, and they now have four beautiful LatAsian children. After serving as a youth pastor and church planter in South Central Los Angeles for fourteen years, Susie continues to teach and preach around the country and serves as a lead co-pastor at Midtown Covenant Church in Sacramento, California.

Angie Kay Hong is a writer, public theologian, speaker, and worship leader. She has a master of divinity degree from Duke University and is a cofounder of Kinship Commons, a liturgy company that creates experiential and transformative gatherings with the aim of the flourishing of marginalized people in view. Angie was formerly a creative director at the Chicago campus of Willow Creek Community Church and has led worship for various churches and conferences, including the annual Christian Community Development Association, the Justice Conference, and the Duke Divinity School Summer Institute for Reconciliation. She has written for *The Atlantic*, *Chalkbeat*, *Christianity Today*, and *Faith and Leadership*.

Nikole Lim is a speaker, educator, and author of the book *Liberation Is Here*. As the founder and international director of Freely in Hope, Nikole has been deeply transformed by the powerful, tenacious, and awe-inspiring stories of survivors. Their audacious dreams have informed her philosophy for a survivor-led approach to community transformation. Nikole graduated with a bachelor's degree in film production from Loyola Marymount University and a master's degree in global leadership from Fuller Theological Seminary. She is a student in embodied contemplative psychotherapy through the Nalanda Institute for Contemplative Science. She is a native of the Bay Area and can often be found buying African fabric on the streets of Nairobi.

Pricelis Perreaux-Dominguez is the founder and CEO of Full Collective and creator of the annual Christian conference in New York City called Sowers

Summit. She is the author of *Being a Sanctuary: The Radical Way for the Body of Christ to Be Sacred, Soft, and Safe* and is currently pursuing a master's degree in biblical and theological studies at Denver Seminary. Pricelis is a Black Latina who lives in New York with her husband and son.

Keisha Polonio is a Belizean therapist, speaker, and abstract artist. For the past twenty years, she has served vulnerable people as a child-welfare case manager, an advocate for survivors of sex trafficking, and a non-profit leader. She now creates space for BIPOC communities to heal one therapy session at a time.

Sara Shaban is a critical/cultural media scholar and assistant professor of journalism and communication at Seattle Pacific University. Her research focuses on the intersections between media, women's social movements, and geopolitics in the Middle East. She published her first book, *Iranian Feminism and Transnational Ethics in Media Discourse*, in 2022.

Patricia A. Taylor is a mother of three, antiracism educator, writer, speaker and podcaster. She is a truth teller and compassionate advocate who has facilitated trips and camps for children and adults seeking deeper understanding in their antiracism journeys and has contributed to the Sesame Street in Communities Organization. Her desire to lead with unwavering empathy and honesty is at the core of her work, which is undergirded by her belief in brown Jesus, loving all our neighbors, and having critical conversations around racial justice that promote active steps toward equity.

PART 1

MATRIARCHS
OF THE
PAST

Caring for myself is not self-indulgence, it is self-preservation, and that is an act of political warfare.

—Audre Lorde

1

Holy and Whole

May God himself, the God who makes everything holy and whole, make you holy and whole, put you together—spirit, soul, and body—and keep you fit for the coming of our Master, Jesus Christ. The One who called you is completely dependable.

—1 Thessalonians 5:23 (Message)

In an age when girl-boss meritocracy and White feminism are glorified at the expense of *all* women flourishing, we have much to learn from the thread of communal renewal weaved through the stories of our minority sisters in history. These image bearers who've gone before us demanded civil and human rights when the status quo failed to address their needs. They cast aside a system not built for them and challenged the norms—and in some cases downright evil—of their time and place. Countless Black, Indigenous, and Women of

Color, as well as those with disabilities, bear a lineage stained by oppression, racism, sexism, othering, and traumas of the very worst kind. Yet our matriarchs and mothers, aunties and abuelas, ammas and ommas embodied goodness and tenacity in their honest quest for survival. So do we. Their spirit of resilience runs through our veins, and like them, we know goodness is our birthright. The One who makes everything holy and whole makes *us* holy and whole, and in turn, we push for wholeness in our world.

Perhaps the matriarchs with complicated backstories have the most for us to glean from, as their very lives were often on the line as they navigated the difficulties that came their way.

In Joshua 2, before the Israelites colonized Jericho, Joshua sent two spies to scope out the land. These spies found protection in the unlikely form of a woman called Rahab. Engaged in the oldest profession and the head of her household, Rahab shrewdly made a deal with the Israelite spies to spare herself and her family in exchange for her aid. Additionally, she prophesied, as Deborah did before her, the Israelites' victory over Canaanite territory. Rahab's unique geolocation on the outskirts of the city, reserved for the lowborn and outcasts, positioned her perfectly to aid the Israelite spies. As someone with a disreputable occupation and no way to rise above her station, she brokered this deal that brought safety and security for herself and her extended family in a time and place when few things could. Her belief in the God of Israel led her to risk everything with this treasonous act, and when Israel conquered Jericho, her female-led household was grafted into the new sociopolitical order of Israel.[1] A

Canaanite woman engaged in prostitution (a triple deficit) is the fearless mouthpiece of what's to come for Israel and is a matriarch named in the lineage of Jesus (Matt. 1:5). Her actions were motivated not by meritocracy or a lick of girl-boss energy but by a fierce commitment to care for herself and her family in a place that did not.

Rahab's account teaches us that our approach to renewal first begins with identifying our nonnegotiable values, what we will and won't tolerate. *That's* self-care. Arguably, self-care equips us for social change. When I refer to self-care, I'm not referring to the $1.5 trillion industry that hawks bubble baths and yoga retreats marketed to us by capitalistic machines who wish to profit from our perceived deficiencies.[2] Rather, it's looking out for ourselves in a world that does not. Author Julia Lee's description of self-care hits the nail on the head. She says that it's "treating yourself as human in a world that dehumanizes you."[3] Self-care is living as worthy of respect and rest simply because you exist and not because you've accomplished something extraordinary to deserve such an existence. Women's health psychiatrist Dr. Pooja Lakshmin says that self-care is a verb, a commitment to live by your guiding principles in your everyday decision-making.[4] It's proactive rather than reactive.[5] Self-care is inherently subjective, and we'd be wise to allow others to grow in their own time and place as they consider their history, culture, and wounds. Self-care for social change is developed when we build healthy boundaries, hold paradoxes, consider what we believe, and evolve in our becoming for the betterment of ourselves and others.

Within our commitment to follow the Creator is a measure of self-denial, but this is not at odds with our actualized self-care. These two things work together to forge an embodied life of deep trust in the Divine and wise decision-making that *centers* the flourishing of our heart, mind, soul, and strength. If we're to love our neighbor as ourselves, as Jesus told his followers in Mark 12, the implied command is to care for ourselves. Rahab knew caring for herself meant bucking societal standards and refusing to honor unjust systems. We aren't promised everything will bend our way because we take care of ourselves and others, and we'll likely never be in a position to broker a deal with foreign spies, but the woman we become along the way—noble and humble, unapologetic and empathetic—that's the woman the world has been waiting for.

PRAYER

God of Rahab,
make me holy and whole.
Giver of Life,
strengthen my spirit, soul, and body.

• • •

DECLARATION

I'm becoming the woman
I've waited for:
noble and humble,
unapologetic and empathetic.

QUESTIONS TO PONDER

- How do you define self-care?
- How can you connect the dots in your own life from self-care to social change?

2

Last at the Cross

And many women were there watching from a distance, who had followed Jesus from Galilee while caring for Him. Among them were Mary Magdalene, Mary the mother of James and Joseph, and the mother of the sons of Zebedee.

—Matthew 27:55–56 (NASB)

What happens when we can't fix another person's pain? When no amount of prayer or protective measures prevents the awful? The unthinkable? The tragic? When the prognosis or plan ends in loss? What then is our obligation to ourselves and those we love?

In the case of the women at the cross, their worst nightmare had become their reality. Their beloved Jesus hung before them, seemingly helpless and clearly in pain. Most of the men had fled out of fear of arrest, imprisonment, or even a death sentence of their own, but not these women; they remained—despite the Romans' willingness to crucify women too. They were in close enough proximity that Jesus was able to address his mother and instruct her on who would take care of her (John 19:26). Although they had nothing to gain and no way to stop the proverbial and physical bleeding, they stayed. Despite the danger to themselves and their inability to help, they would not leave Jesus's side. In their rabbi's agony, they remained actively present.

Each woman had witnessed the kindness, compassion, and grace of Jesus. They were no stranger to his miracles or might, but in the dark of that day their hopes faded along with the life of the man on that wooden cross. I can't imagine anyone would have judged them for leaving his side, but that wasn't who they were. Before they were women of the resurrection, they were women unafraid of standing with Jesus in his darkest hour at Golgotha. Although Sunday morning was around the corner, Friday first took a heavy toll. The women at the cross weren't afraid of remaining present, of feeling every sorrow-laden emotion, as Jesus suffered and died.

I vividly remember lying on the floor next to a friend whose father died in a freak accident, my arm resting on her back as she let out guttural screams. I willed myself not to say a word but simply remained by her side. When my closest friend of twenty years anticipated the upcoming nuptials between her ex-husband and his new fiancé, I laid next to her as she fell asleep—my presence a reminder she wasn't alone on the night of his wedding. When a dear friend miscarried in her second trimester of pregnancy, my only offering was arms wrapped around her shoulders as she wept. The practice of simply being present versus attempting to pacify the pain of others acknowledges our helplessness to assuage their suffering. It's emotionally, mentally, and physically taxing yet honors the personhood of another. While encouraging words have their place, Ecclesiastes 3:7 tells us there is a time to be silent and a time to speak, and I felt my physical presence was the best comfort I could offer.

Staying present is indeed a holy act that forms us into the likeness of Christ. Former professor of pastoral care at Fuller Theological Seminary David Augsburger shares, "Presence is not a method; it is embodying grace, incarnating love; it is fleshing out the steadfast love of God." He continues:

> Out of our experience of God's faithfulness, we learn how to be faithful to one another in our willingness to be present with all our vulnerabilities. Our presence to one another mediates God's presence to us. The abiding certainty of God's presence is not and cannot be a substitute for our presence—being the face of God to each other. God's compassionate presence is mediated in the caring presence of God's people. Just as we know that nothing—pain, suffering, even death—can separate us from the compassionate love of God, so we stubbornly refuse to let anything intervene in our presence with those who suffer.[1]

We serve as the proxy for divine comfort and care when we remain actively present in a cruel world overcome by harm and loss. The late theologian Wilbert Shenk once wrote, "We are not free to choose or reject a theology of presence. Presence as incarnation is fundamental to all witness."[2] Our embodied presence may be the only Jesus others encounter, and our life in Christ blossoms as we root ourselves in the here and now, being vulnerable alongside of others.

As the women at the cross remained actively present, may we remain present to those precious to us in times of tragedy. May we recognize, as the apostle Paul did, that to live *is* Christ (Phil. 1:21). I pray that those we encounter meet the kind, compassionate, and caring Christ within us. May we humanize and honor the personhood of another while recognizing how near and actively present the Divine is to us.

PRAYER

God of the Present Women,
give me energy to be present for others.
God Who Is Endlessly Present with Us,
I take comfort in your nearness.

• • •

DECLARATION

I will practice active presence
with beloved image bearers.
I receive the kind and comforting presence
from the One who loves me.

• • •

QUESTIONS TO PONDER

- In what situations or relationships do you struggle to stay actively present?
- Who has offered you active presence? How has that shaped your understanding of self? Of the Divine?

3

Know Better, Do Better

PATRICIA A. TAYLOR

> He has shown you, O mortal, what is good.
>   And what does the LORD require of you?
> To act justly and to love mercy
>   and to walk humbly with your God.
>
> —Micah 6:8

When we know better, we do better. This idea doesn't depend or change based on our personality, on what we have or don't have, or on our place and space—nor should it. As followers of Jesus, we evolve, we grow, we act justly, love mercy, and humbly journey with our God. We don't finish where we started, and we can find ourselves immersed in the grand story of redemption along the way.

Jean Wiley understood this and unapologetically set out to make a positive impact in her community. Born in 1942 and raised in Baltimore, Maryland, Jean was a brilliant civil rights activist who began her storied career of leadership and change as a young student at Morgan State College (now Morgan State University) in Baltimore when the sit-ins began in 1960. When speaking of her participation in the sit-ins at age seventeen, she stated that they seemed like the perfect thing to do, so she, along with many other students from fellow Black colleges and universities, "jumped right in."[1] She later became involved with the Student Nonviolent Coordinating Committee (SNCC) and the Northern Student Movement (NSM), while she continued her activism as a faculty member at Tuskegee Institute (now university) in Alabama. She sought to expand minds to embrace possibility, and her house became a crash pad for SNCC activists who passed through town on their way to their next organizing event. It was here that she taught the likes of Sammy Younge Jr. and Ruby Sales, and she was just getting started.

Participating in this movement came with subjection to constant hostility, arrests, and threats against the lives of those who dared to march, protest, and organize. There was the real possibility of being murdered for insisting that Black lives deserve belonging in every space in society without recourse or repercussions. Even when violence was leveled against them (as with Younge Jr., who was killed at the tender age of twenty-one for using the "Whites-only" bathroom at a gas station in Tuskegee), Jean and others dedicated to the cause pressed on.

Making progress for the greater good even in the face of loss of life takes a seemingly otherworldly level of commitment, fortitude, and belief, yet Jean didn't seem to entertain lingering doubts or questions. She was acutely aware of what needed to be done and resolutely set out to do it.

Jean was a witness to her own family's struggle with segregation during her childhood. Her father was a painter, along with two of her uncles, and for fifteen years they tried to gain entry into a labor union that would offer more opportunities and higher pay. Despite their efforts, they were categorically denied participation in a system that was structured to prevent Black individuals from gaining equal footing. As a daughter, she watched her father become worn down trying to fight injustice. As a Black woman, she took up the fight as her own.

In an interview in 2001, Jean spoke of the lack of freedom of movement while living through segregation and how that affected her family and her psyche: "*You can't*, I grew up hearing. *You can't. You can't do this. You can't go to the symphony. You can't go to the library. You can't go to the swimming pool. You can't go to that park, no*."[2] With so many "nos" thrown in her direction everywhere she turned, she was yearning for a way to say yes to herself and yes to the fight for the freedom of Black people. This yes came when she was that young college student (not even of legal age) who participated in her first sit-in and thought, "Oh, but I *can* do something about this."[3]

The personal became political.

Her own experiences formed her conviction that what her family and countless others faced was inhumane and immoral, and she acted with the belief that there had to be a better way.

Over the span of her lifetime, Jean Wiley's work evolved and took her to different places and spaces. She held positions at the University of the District of

Columbia, the Center for Black Education, and the University of California at Berkeley (to name a few). In these locations and others, she was a formative influence who passed on her fervor for justice to others.

Under Jean's tutelage at Tuskegee Institute, Ruby Sales was first inspired by the writing of civil rights activist James Baldwin. Sales, a living legend of the civil rights movement, is now a nationally recognized human rights activist, a public theologian, and the founder and executive director of Spirit House Project. This nonprofit uses the arts, education, action, and research to bring diverse people together for the work of social and economic justice and spiritual formation.

While we all have our own choices to make, one can't help but wonder at how the actions of one can influence the actions of many and what we'd all be missing if Jean Wiley and so many of our matriarchs who fought for equality had chosen to sit on the sidelines instead.

As a child, Jean was motivated by what she observed, and living in a segregated America as a Black female ensured she would have her own stories to tell. As a young person, she knew what she had to do. She knew when it was her time to jump right in.

For those who are marginalized and live with experiences of oppression, there may at times be a clearly defined path as to how and when to jump into the fight, as there was with Jean. But acting in the name of what's just and right for all image bearers, as Micah 6:8 describes, is a mandate for all of us.

Once we know better it really is incumbent on each of us to do better, and in spite of whatever fears, hesitations, and obstacles lie before us, may we always carry the knowledge that God is with us in the doing.

PRAYER

God of Jean Wiley,
may we seek to act justly, love mercy,
and walk humbly in your name;
may we commit to jumping right in, with
our hands, feet, words, and actions;
may we believe that better is possible and
act in ways to help our collective liberation
and flourishing become a reality.

• • •

DECLARATION

I will act not only for myself but also for my neighbor.
I do not have to experience oppression to
fight for freedom for the oppressed.
I am unshakable in my commitment
to advocating for progress.
I know that God is with me in the doing.

• • •

QUESTIONS TO PONDER

- What steps have you taken to be an active participant in the flourishing of your neighborhood and community?

- What is your strategy to stay engaged when you are feeling weary?

- If you have not taken any steps, what plans can you make today to get started?

4

Mothers of the Movement

God has blessed you above all women.

—Luke 1:42 (NLT)

In our journey of faith, we'd be wise to remember that our whole being, our whole story, is considered and cared for by the Divine. We are treasured, and we needn't divide our loyalties to walk in the will of God; our whole self is welcome.

Mary knew this.

The years of waiting were over. The cries and anguish from all God's creatures had not been ignored, and a redemption plan was in motion. But it wouldn't take place without the active, embodied participation of a woman who was willing to become a mother. Neither a queen nor a duchess was chosen for the role, not a war hero or ancient celebrity. Amid political unrest, rampant poverty, and a refugee crisis in Palestine, a teenage girl from the other side of the tracks was handpicked by the Divine to carry liberation by way of her womb.

Mary's consent to the assignment of heaven bore potential real-world ramifications of harm. First-century law stated that whether betrothed or married, those found guilty of adultery were subject to death. Never mind that sexual assault was commonplace in the ancient world, where women possessed minimal rights. Women held little bodily autonomy and were betrothed as young as twelve years old. Stories of the sexual subjugation of women are threaded throughout the Old Testament, from Hagar to Bathsheba to Tamar. Mary's first act in defiance of this pattern was to carry a baby, and no man took advantage of her body to do so. She willingly challenged the law to mother a movement *before* Joseph chose to continue with their wedding plans.

Hurriedly, the Scriptures indicate, freshly pregnant Mary flees Galilee and travels roughly a hundred miles to Judah to lodge with her elder cousin Elizabeth, who, despite her advanced age, is six months into her own surprise pregnancy. Two first-time mamas, a poor teenage girl and her geriatric cousin, are about to birth the leaders of the liberation. But before they do, we witness solidarity. One woman shows up for another.

Luke 1:39–45 reads,

> A few days later Mary hurried to the hill country of Judea, to the town where Zechariah lived. She entered the house and greeted Elizabeth. At the sound of Mary's greeting, Elizabeth's child leaped within her, and Elizabeth was filled with the Holy Spirit.

> Elizabeth gave a glad cry and exclaimed to Mary,
> "God has blessed you above all women, and your child
> is blessed. Why am I so honored, that the mother of
> my Lord should visit me? When I heard your greeting,
> the baby in my womb jumped for joy. You are blessed
> because you believed that the Lord would do what he
> said." (NLT)

Filled with the Spirit, Elizabeth doesn't give Mary side-eye or show even a tinge of jealousy toward her younger kin, but without hesitation she exclaims, "God has blessed you above all women."

This refrain, this blessing, spoken over iconic women in Israelite history, was extended to a lowly servant girl who was destined to fight in the resistance not with a weapon but with her womb.[1] Memorably spoken by Deborah to Jael (Judg. 5:24) after Jael secured an Israelite victory with a tent peg to the temple of the enemy, the blessing spoke of empowerment and agency against the backdrop of a patriarchal society. Theologian Kelley Nikondeha notes, "Elizabeth's reprisal comes as a glorious twist, since Mary will embody nonviolent participation in the advent of God's peace. And Elizabeth's verse will add a new understanding of deliverance, opening space for women in the future to engage tumultuous times and to effect change. Everyone who heard the song's beginning would assume they knew how it ended. But Elizabeth and Mary, under the auspices of the Spirit, understood the song as pointing in a new direction."[2] While Deborah and Jael delivered death to usher in victory, Mary and Elizabeth would, in a reversal, usher in life to bring victory.

For the mothers of this kingdom movement, their willingness to participate in God's grand plan was their act of resistance, and they were in it together. They had each other, their voices, and a commitment to protect the vulnerable people in their midst. Even more striking is the confidence Elizabeth's encouragement stokes within Mary. After a show of solidarity, in which Elizabeth honors the life and role of her young cousin, Mary responds with a song—the Magnificat. Lyrics of defiance and ancient proclamations of triumph were unheard of from poor girls who held no power, yet that's what Luke records.

> Oh, how my soul praises the Lord.
>> How my spirit rejoices in God my Savior!
> For he took notice of his lowly servant girl,
>> and from now on all generations will call me
>> blessed.
> For the Mighty One is holy,
>> and he has done great things for me.
> He shows mercy from generation to generation
>> to all who fear him.
> His mighty arm has done tremendous things!
>> He has scattered the proud and haughty
>> ones.
> He has brought down princes from their thrones
>> and exalted the humble.
> He has filled the hungry with good things
>> and sent the rich away with empty hands.
> He has helped his servant Israel
>> and remembered to be merciful.
> For he made this promise to our ancestors,
>> to Abraham and his children forever. (Luke
>> 1:46–55 NLT)

Mary and Elizabeth chose to mother in a destabilized region under the weight of oppressive rule, which was no small task. They melded their political, social, and familial responsibilities with their faith. May we do the same. Like them, may we carry on with radical tenderness and tenacity in our own unpredictable time and place, where there is no short supply of heaviness and heartache.

PRAYER

God of Mother Mary,
grant me the confidence to endure this season.
God of Mother Elizabeth,
blossom within me a spirit of solidarity.

• • •

DECLARATION

I am not alone.
I stand in the shadow of strong women.

• • •

QUESTIONS TO PONDER

- What have you deemed a limitation in your life that could very well be the key to your liberation story?
- Who needs your solidarity?
- Who needs your encouragement?

5

Dreams of the Matriarchs

ASHLEE EILAND

"In the last days," God says,
    "I will pour out my Spirit on all people.
Your sons and daughters will prophesy. . . .
Even on my servants, both men and women,
    I will pour out my Spirit in those days,
    and they will prophesy.
I will show wonders in the heavens above
    and signs on the earth below."

—Acts 2:17–19

Our dreams are equal-opportunity employers, bestowed on boys and girls, men and women alike. They come in all shapes and sizes, all colors and types. Some outlive and outlast us, while some order our days. And for many of us, *we* are the dream—the dream of our matriarchs.

As a girl, Katherine Johnson didn't just dream of translucent, imaginary cloud bubbles. She dreamed of the great expanse of space: stars and moons and galaxies. And she dreamed of these things in numbers.

From early childhood, Katherine was known to be a counter of things, a sharp girl with a sharp mind who would eventually use the sharp, precise edge of a slide rule to aid in the calculations she and other NASA mathematicians (or "computers" as they were called at the time) worked out by hand. They were the calculations that would get astronauts to the moon and back without error or catastrophe.

But that skill did not find itself easily celebrated. When she was younger, her hometown's segregated education system allowed Black children to receive instruction only through sixth grade. Katherine's father, Joshua Coleman, relocated his family 125 miles away to Institute, West Virginia, so his four children could learn with fewer barriers. It was here that Katherine attended a high school program connected to a historically Black institution that is now West Virginia State University. She was ten years old when she began that program and did something that was surely beyond her ancestors' wildest dreams; she graduated at fourteen.

In 1952, Katherine found out that Langley was hiring Black female mathematicians. The hiring requirements for Black female computers were different, however, from those for White women applying for the same jobs. Black women were required to have college degrees and a high GPA, while White women were not. Katherine easily met the requirements, despite this biased and unfair hiring system, and began work at Langley Memorial Aeronautical Laboratory (which eventually became a NASA field center) in June 1953. Though her work was valuable, Katherine and the other computers were not publicly recognized. They worked behind the scenes, navigating barriers that both subtly and explicitly served to alienate and marginalize them.

In an ironic twist, the unfair hiring system eventually worked in Katherine's favor. Because the Black women needed college degrees, they were called on more frequently than the White computers by their male engineer counterparts. Shortly after Katherine started working at Langley, an engineer walked into the space where the Black computers were working. He needed help. Katherine's boss, knowing she was one of the best—if not *the* best—computers, suggested Katherine join him. It's said that Katherine followed this engineer into a room full of White men. They gave her a set of calculations that had stumped them. Looking them over carefully, Katherine quickly caught an error. From that point forward, Katherine's work was held in high regard by her male colleagues. Eventually, this woman who used to count church steps and stars as a girl submitted a report that included the calculated path that would determine where a spacecraft could safely land. It was the first report of its kind authored by a woman.[1]

Sometimes being the embodied dream of our matriarchs is not about instant shine in the spotlight. Sometimes *being* a dream—versus just *having* a dream—looks like opposition and the sacrifice of traveling many miles from home. It looks like confidence in what we've been given in the way of skill and gifts passed down through bloodline and legacy, not just confidence in the container within which those gifts are contained.

The bigger dream isn't stifled by barriers or by signs put up to keep us out of certain spaces.

The bigger dream is the miracle of our very lives, that despite opposition we exist. And we get to decide if we will allow the barriers to conceal our gifts. We get to decide if we will let the dream of our ancestors die because those in power do not see us.

Acts 2 paints a picture that defies first-century barriers. Peter addresses a crowd that has just received a filling of the Holy Spirit. Men and women from all over are celebrating wildly when this dramatic outpouring takes place. Some look on this encounter and question what is actually happening. Are these people drunk? But Peter knows better than to allow the moment to pass without pointing out the embodiment of a prophet's dream. Joel's prophecy (Joel 2:28–32) is being lived out at that very moment. Gifts are being given and used, unimpeded by the limitations placed on them by the religious and political powers of the day: "I will pour out my Spirit on all people. Your sons and daughters will prophesy. . . . Even on my servants, both men and women, I will pour out my Spirit in those days" (Acts 2:17–18). Catherine Kroeger and Mary Evans highlight the radical implications of this dream coming to fruition: "Prophecy was less to do with prediction of the future and more to do with acting as the mouthpiece of God. . . . Women, equally with men, are equipped by the Spirit in this new phase of the kingdom."[2]

If we are our matriarchs' dreams, we will live like we know this. Dreams see the barriers and enter through the threshold of restricted access anyway. Dreams are content being behind the scenes, still calculating and creating with greatness. Dreams know this world is not all there is, that there is a place beyond, one where gifts have a home and cannot be destroyed. Dreams aren't just an idea or even a skill. They're people.

The dream . . . is you. You who rocket into the unknown and come back to tell the story alongside the other saints. You who are the fulfillment of a hope, a holy prophecy.

As dreams ourselves, we as women hold equal authority to tell of the work of the greatest plan, one that broke the barriers of heaven to ensure we would not be destroyed. That plan was not the outcome of our own ideas or gifts but the work of a person, fully God and fully human, showing love for all humanity.

As our matriarchs' dreams, we are part of a cosmic plan.

No system can ever defy its goodness.

It is the plan of God's salvation.

PRAYER

God of Dreams and Prophecies,
help me see myself as the embodiment of hope.
God Who Broke Barriers,
give me the courage to steward the gifts
you've given me with confidence,
that I may joyfully take part in your holy plan.

• • •

DECLARATION

I will gratefully use my gifts.
I will disempower barriers created to limit me.
I will serve alongside others to
tell of God's salvation.

QUESTIONS TO PONDER

- What are the gifts you've been given?
- What barriers have prevented you from seeing yourself as the dream of your matriarchs?
- What conditions have you instituted as prerequisites to using your gifts? How can you put on humility?
- How have you been created to take part in God's plan of salvation for the world?

6

Birthright

Give us property along with the rest of our relatives.
—Numbers 27:4 (NLT)

Contrary to popular belief, we aren't limited to un-equivocal, one-right-way thinking as we seek the full-ness of Christ. Often we operate in the gray. And as the intelligent, creative, and resourceful women of convic-tion that we are, maybe that's not a bad thing.

Five fatherless daughters named in Numbers 27 did just that; they laid claim to what was theirs while navi-gating a system that failed to bear them in mind. They could have kept to themselves and seethed silently over their erasure, angered but not incensed enough to raise a fuss. After all, what could they do? They were young women, descendants of Egyptian slavery, their father had passed, and decrees of their day favored sons, not daughters. After a census was taken to count male heirs to determine the portion of their inheritance, the five sisters saw property rights awarded only to sons in exile over twenty years old—to the new generation of Israeli men who would lead the Hebrew tribes into Jericho, the promised land. Daughters had no such benefit. Written by men to benefit men, the ruling impacted hundreds of thousands of people and their future stability, but if you were brotherless you were cut out of the deal and left without assets.

Mahlah, Noah, Hoglah, Milcah, and Tirzah, the five determined and diplomatic daughters of Zelophehad, challenged the new decree. With confidence, Scripture indicates, the sisters left their tent and made their way to the entrance of the Tabernacle to bring their petition before Moses and company. Intent on claiming their right not with fists but with facts, the sisters shared their personal history and how the law failed to address brotherless daughters of Israel.

Numbers 27:1–8 tells of their advocacy:

> One day a petition was presented by the daughters of Zelophehad—Mahlah, Noah, Hoglah, Milcah, and Tirzah. Their father, Zelophehad, was a descendant of Hepher son of Gilead, son of Makir, son of Manasseh, son of Joseph. These women stood before Moses, Eleazar the priest, the tribal leaders, and the entire community at the entrance of the Tabernacle. "Our father died in the wilderness," they said. "He was not among Korah's followers, who rebelled against the LORD; he died because of his own sin. But he had no sons. Why should the name of our father disappear from his clan just because he had no sons? Give us property along with the rest of our relatives."
>
> So Moses brought their case before the LORD. And the LORD replied to Moses, "The claim of the

daughters of Zelophehad is legitimate. You must give them a grant of land along with their father's relatives. Assign them the property that would have been given to their father. And give the following instructions to the people of Israel: If a man dies and has no son, then give his inheritance to his daughters." (NLT)

In their appeal to the male leaders, the sisters made a case for their inclusion in honor of their father's lineage. Zelophehad followed Moses as he fled Egypt, crossed the Red Sea, camped in the wilderness, witnessed God's provision for years, and didn't rebel when others did. Upon his death, he didn't deserve to be forgotten simply because he had daughters, and since the acknowledgment of a family name was directly correlated with land ownership, the daughters wanted their due.

Brenda Bacon, an educator at the Schechter Institute of Jewish Studies, notes,

> Their argument, "Let not our father's name be lost to his clan," was one that could find a sympathetic response in the ears of the male leaders. In using this tactic, the women displayed an understanding of the constraints of the patriarchal society in which they lived. Rather than present an unqualified demand that daughters inherit equally with sons, they limited their demand to cases in which there are no sons. Their diplomacy enabled them to get the attention of Moses, for their demand was not a threat to the patriarchal order, but rather in accordance with the male concern for continuity.[1]

The five sisters worked within the unfair system to reveal negligence at the hands of those charged with their survival. Their plan succeeded.

Our twenty-first-century assumptions of what constitutes flourishing may assume it was one step forward and two steps back for women of their day; after all, the sisters didn't plead for equality between men and women but rather for care only in the absence of male heirs. Nevertheless, Mahlah, Noah, Hoglah, Milcah, and Tirzah sought to survive in a world where men overlooked their dignity and needs. They shrewdly challenged the new rule book and advocated for themselves. Moses didn't balk or backpedal when the sisters asked for what should have been their right to begin with. He went before God, and God, true to Godself, agreed with the sisters and made clear to Moses that they were to receive their inheritance. Their birthright. The sisters believed they were worthy long before they were acknowledged by Moses or anyone else in the tabernacle.

Birthrights that give claim to a family's inheritance in biblical history are reserved for firstborn sons, never firstborn daughters, let alone second-, third-, fourth-, and even fifthborn daughters. Yet in the coming but not-yet way of the kingdom, God aligns with five female image bearers to upend a patriarchal practice that doesn't recognize the feminine as worthy, let alone acknowledge their land rights.

The book of Judges offers us another account of a woman petitioning for rights: Acsah, the only daughter of Caleb. The same Caleb who spied on the promised land and gave a positive report to Moses (Josh. 14:5–8) promised his daughter to whoever could conquer Kiriath-sepher, an inhabited land they sought to claim. Wouldn't you know it, his nephew Othniel finished the job. As a prize for his conquest, he took his cousin as his wife.

Caleb said, "I will give my daughter Acsah in marriage to the one who attacks and captures Kiriath-sepher." Othniel, the son of Caleb's younger brother, Kenaz, was the one who conquered it, so Acsah became Othniel's wife.

When Acsah married Othniel, she urged him to ask her father for a field. As she got down off her donkey, Caleb asked her, "What's the matter?"

She said, "Let me have another gift. You have already given me land in the Negev; now please give me springs of water, too." So Caleb gave her the upper and lower springs. (Judg. 1:12–15 NLT)

In Acsah's cousin-husband situation, she displayed an unwavering commitment to her birthright despite a clear lack of bodily autonomy. Othniel's dowry from his uncle was not enough for Acsah. She asked for the gift of the springs, likely to irrigate the land already given. She counted herself among the descendants of Caleb, as deserving as her three brothers, and asked for a part of the family inheritance. Numbers 14:24 reads, "But my servant Caleb has a different attitude than the others have. He has remained loyal to me, so I will bring him into the land he explored. His descendants will possess their full share of that land" (NLT). Acsah claimed her birthright and pressed her father to give her what was rightfully hers.

Like Zelophehad's daughters and Acsah, we operate within systems that are not always mindful of women's rights, dignity, and agency. But like our biblical matriarchs, we can stand in alignment with the Divine and work within dysfunctional spaces, recognizing that our advancements don't solve all of life's issues but do offer some reprieve. Our small gains within an imperfect system might feel like a consolation prize when we hoped for more, but they're something to work with—a shred of movement in the right direction. It sets a precedent for those coming after us to look for a work-around and ask for more. To imagine new ways of existing just as our matriarchs did.

PRAYER

God of Zelophehad's Daughters,
grant me wisdom to advocate for myself and others.
God of Acsah,
give me the audacity to see myself as you do.

• • •

DECLARATION

What I deserve is not defined by others
but is given by the God who loves me.

• • •

QUESTIONS TO PONDER

- When you think of your birthright, what comes to mind?
- If you've struggled with measuring others by what you think you deserve, how can you begin to think differently?

7

Healing

"Daughter," he said to her, "your faith has made you well. Go in peace."

—Luke 8:48

From our first day on this earth, wherever we go, our bodies take us there. For better or for worse, they're ours to steward, to accept as they are. They have experienced much, and they've certainly "kept the score."[1] In a world that measures our worth by whether we fall within socially constructed norms of "fitness"—both in mind and body—healing can be hard to find.

In forced seclusion for over a decade and weak from hemorrhaging blood, the nameless woman identified only by her malady in Luke 8 is deemed ritually impure and isolated from her community. She has tried all the popular methods and remedies in hopes of a cure, but they left her broke and alone. I can only imagine the intense loneliness and anxiety that would plague a suffering woman left on her own in a patriarchal society. Although she was robbed of belonging, of touch, of value, we witness embodied healing when she seeks out Jesus. At some point in her journey, she concludes that the Healer from Nazareth is caring and capable. While she might have hoped to gain an audience with Jesus, she only manages to touch the hem of his robe. In an instant, everything changes. Her ailment is healed. Her worth is recognized.

After Jesus questions the crowd, likely asking who had touched him in a rhetorical way, he listens as the no-longer-bleeding woman confesses her actions. He famously responds by calling her "daughter" (Luke 8:48). She isn't dragged from the crowd and thrown to the side, nor is she berated for touching a holy man. Instead, the woman who has been without a family for twelve years due to circumstances outside her control is addressed with familial endearment by a man she doesn't even know. He could have commended her faith without healing her body, but it was her bodily trauma that he cared for—freeing her from forced isolation *as well as* her physical ailment. Her entire being is precious to him. Because of his empathy, his safe presence, and his divinity, her place in her community is restored and her body is healed. Therapist K.J. Ramsey claims, "Trauma isn't healed by memorizing verses a biblical counselor gives as homework. It's healed thru the embodied experience of restoring safety."[2] Of all that we can glean from Jesus and the hemorrhaging woman's exchange, the safety he offered tops the list.

Her Healer knew that he too would soon experience divine healing. Philippians 2:6–11 reads,

> Though he was God,
>> he did not think of equality with God
>> as something to cling to.
> Instead, he gave up his divine privileges;
>> he took the humble position of a slave
>> and was born as a human being.
> When he appeared in human form,
>> he humbled himself in obedience to God
>> and died a criminal's death on a cross.
> Therefore, God elevated him to the place of
>>> highest honor
>> and gave him the name above all other
>> names,
> that at the name of Jesus every knee should
>> bow,
>> in heaven and on earth and under the earth,
> and every tongue declare that Jesus Christ is
>> Lord,
>> to the glory of God the Father. (NLT)

The Creator could have modeled wholeness in myriad ways, but he chose a body: blood, guts, and bones. The One who hung the stars and filled the seas also felt the crunch of earth under his feet, sweat drip from his brow, the wind beat his cheek. Born to a young mother during a refugee crisis, his early life threatened by a murderous leader, he was fully present to the realities of his time and the accompanying emotional, mental, and physical trauma. In his crucifixion, he felt the sting of thorns pressed into his temple, the burn from the whip on his back, and the mocking taunts from those who wanted him dead. His divinity was not divorced from his humanity. He endured traumatic events as we have. He understands and makes space for our healing, for our becoming within our bodies.

To attend to our traumas is to acknowledge our vulnerabilities. Sadly, when women speak of the emotional, physical, and psychological pain that torments them—from their frontal cortex to the tips of their toes—they are sometimes treated like they don't *know* their own bodies, as if their experiences are innately untrustworthy. But we know ourselves. Our minds. Our bodies. Our spirits.

Perhaps coming home to ourselves is a restorative healing journey unique to each of us. A bodily affair, soul never separated from sinew. We smell, touch, taste, see, and hear our way to renewal. And like the bleeding woman and her Healer, we embody healing as faithfulness to our becoming our truest selves.

PRAYER

God of the Hemorrhaging Woman,
restore and resurrect the broken pieces of me.
God Who Calls Us Daughter,
may my wounds make way for wholeness.

• • •

DECLARATION

I'm coming home to myself:
embodying healing as faithfulness
to becoming my truest self.

QUESTIONS TO PONDER

- Have you limited the idea of healing to remedies or cures?
- How can you reframe healing as faithfulness?

8

Prayers of Our Mothers

SUSIE GAMEZ

Early on the first day of the week, while it was still dark, Mary Magdalene went to the tomb and saw that the stone had been removed from the entrance.

—John 20:1

Our desperate prayers often lead us to thin places, places where we can break barriers and do things differently.

I don't know if the believers in South Korea who first adopted the practice of early morning prayer were familiar with Celtic Christian spirituality, but when I read about the Celtic notion of thin places—that is, "a place where the boundary between heaven and earth is especially thin"[1]—it made me think of *saebyuk gido*, or dawn prayer.

Many Koreans love to pray in the mountains at dawn. In mountaintop areas the air is thin, and this physical thinness may help one feel as though spiritual barriers are thinner as well. I've heard that graveyards or cemeteries can also have this kind of effect. As you walk through a cemetery, you are reminded of the thin space between life and death.

I wonder if the time right before dawn, when it's no longer night but not yet day, is a thin place too. It may help us feel as though time is less of a barrier, challenge, or distraction.

If you grew up with the Spirit-filled, early-morning prayers led by Korean immigrant parents like mine, you probably know the *Jooyuh* drill. You wake up at what we ironically call an "ungodly" hour—4:30, maybe 5:00 a.m.—and when the prayer meeting starts, in one voice, all together, you say *Jooyuh*, which means "Lord," three times. On the first prayer, you start with a lower decibel *Jooyuh*, one that comes out almost like a breath prayer. On the next one, you get a little louder, with a little more urgency and a little more fervor. The last *JOOOYUHHHH* is said loud and held long with a good amount of angst and desperation. And then all heaven breaks loose in the sound of *tongsong gido* (one voice prayer). Everyone is praying out loud all at once, and you enter into the collective lament and supplication of a people who are familiar with *Han*.

What is *Han*? There's no English word that fully captures it. It's a deeply internalized grief, rage, sorrow, regret, and all things inexpressible in words carried by a people whose history is bound by invasion, oppression, colonialization, trauma, erasure, war, and division.

Whenever I got dragged out to one of these early morning prayer meetings, I remember feeling distracted and even annoyed. I told my umma (mother) that I couldn't concentrate on praying with all the noise. She laughed and said, "*Nuh ajik mohlasuh geulae.*" ("It's because you don't know yet.") She was right.

I still don't know how to pray like she does. It takes practice (not that prayer should be performative), but praying as my umma does requires a rehearsed regimen of kneeling, bowing, and seeking the presence of God while feeling naked, vulnerable, and needy. Earnest prayer requires us to be honest about and aware of our humanity, anxiety, sorrow, anger, and fear. Prayer and seeking the Lord also require intentionality—a 4:30 a.m. before I open my corner store at 8:00 a.m. for a fourteen-hour workday type of intentionality. An "early on the first day of the week, while it was still dark" kind of intentionality. My mother told me that if I didn't know what to pray for, it can be beneficial to just sit quietly and listen. And if you need to, just say *Jooyuh*. Sit with the hope and expectation that the Holy Spirit might open your eyes to see something different.

When she went to the tomb where Jesus was buried, Mary Magdalene expected to find a dead body. But "early on the first day of the week, while it was still dark, Mary Magdalene went to the tomb and saw that the stone had been removed from the entrance" (John 20:1). She did not find what she expected to see, but as she continued to seek after the Lord, in her intentional, desperate time of seeking within a "thin" space and time, the Lord opened her eyes to see something different.

When most people think of Jesus's faithful followers, the twelve men who were called Jesus's disciples are likely the first to come to mind. But contrary to cultural norms, many women followed Jesus, supported his ministry, and shared the good news. Mary Magdalene was an earnest follower of Jesus. Her powerful realization that she had seen things others hadn't is recorded in John:

> Now Mary stood outside the tomb crying. As she wept, she bent over to look into the tomb and saw two angels in white, seated where Jesus' body had been, one at the head and the other at the foot.
>
> They asked her, "Woman, why are you crying?"
>
> "They have taken my Lord away," she said, "and I don't know where they have put him." At this, she turned around and saw Jesus standing there, but she did not realize that it was Jesus.
>
> He asked her, "Woman, why are you crying? Who is it you are looking for?"
>
> Thinking he was the gardener, she said, "Sir, if you have carried him away, tell me where you have put him, and I will get him."
>
> Jesus said to her, "Mary."
>
> She turned toward him and cried out in Aramaic, "Rabboni!" (which means "Teacher").
>
> Jesus said, "Do not hold on to me, for I have not yet ascended to the Father. Go instead to my brothers and tell them, 'I am ascending to my Father and your Father, to my God and your God.'"
>
> Mary Magdalene went to the disciples with the news: "I have seen the Lord!" And she told them that he had said these things to her. (John 20:11–18)

Mary Magdalene was the first to see the resurrected Christ. Mary, along with other women, witnessed the death of Jesus. They were also the first to witness the resurrection and the first to be commissioned to go and tell others about the risen Christ. We live in a world that erects thick barriers to obstruct people on the margins like Mary Magdalene, or my immigrant mom. Perhaps this is what drives women like them to earnestly seek out thin spaces and times. They hear the invitation to seek out a Savior and Liberator who breaks down barriers and invites them to see (and do) something different. May we go and do likewise.

PRAYER

God of Our Ummas,
We cry *Jooyuh. Jooyuh. Jooyuh.*
When I don't have any other words to speak,
help me to call on you.

• • •

DECLARATION

Like Mary Magdalene,
and other women who participated in
the salvation and liberation of others,
I will invite others to seek out thin spaces and times,
so that we may see and do differently.

• • •

QUESTIONS TO PONDER

- What does a thin space or time look like for you?
- What can you do to cultivate more thin spaces or times for yourself and others?

PART 2

HOLY ENDURANCE

I love how the women in scripture aren't so much "obedient" as they are honest and real and characterized by love—for themselves, their people, and in response to their God.

—Kat Armas

9

Advocates for Rest

> For I brought you out of Egypt
>   and redeemed you from slavery.
> I sent Moses, Aaron, and Miriam to help
>   you.
>
> —Micah 6:4 (NLT)

Rest should not have to be earned, as if it's a reward for hard work or toil. No. Rest is necessary to thrive, to endure, to simply exist. Sadly, oppressive leaders and systems have often withheld rest as collateral, an asset given only when their agenda is fulfilled. Thankfully, history is filled with advocates pushing for rest, refusing to play a game that's rigged.

Moses's big sister Miriam is one of them: an advocate for rest.

In Exodus 2, following along the water's edge, Miriam kept a close watch on her baby brother as he floated tucked in his makeshift boat of papyrus reeds. Her mother, Jochebed, had sent her infant son, innocent but hunted, down the Nile River in hopes of rescue, and big sister Miriam would be sure of it. Miriam then spied an Egyptian princess lift him from the water and determine his Hebrew origin, for who would float a three-month-old baby down the Nile except for a desperate mother who feared keeping him would end in death? After the princess's discovery, Miriam approached the royal with a proposition at just the right time. With her offer to find a Hebrew wet nurse for the orphaned baby, Miriam not only secured financial provision for her family but also reunited mother and baby. Even though she was likely not even twelve years old, Miriam was assertive and helpful, and it wouldn't be the last time she was a voice of reason and resistance for her younger brother at the water's edge.

Years later, when Miriam partnered with her brothers, Moses and Aaron, as they sought freedom for their people, the same resolve is seen along the parted waters of the Red Sea. Victoriously, she co-led the rescue of not just one beloved image bearer but of thousands. Born into slavery but not bound by expectations, she dared to prophetically co-lead a migration journey as Israel's advocate for rest.

After waves crashed over enemy chariots, the Israelites celebrated what had previously seemed impossible, and Miriam danced with gratitude to the God of Israel, their rescuer.

> When Pharaoh's horses, chariots, and charioteers rushed into the sea, the LORD brought the water crashing down on them. But the people of Israel had walked through the middle of the sea on dry ground!

Then Miriam the prophet, Aaron's sister, took a tambourine and led all the women as they played their tambourines and danced. And Miriam sang this song:

> Sing to the LORD,
>   for he has triumphed gloriously;
> he has hurled both horse and rider
>   into the sea. (Exod. 15:19–21 NLT)

Miriam and the others dared to believe they weren't mere beasts of burden useful only for the advancement of the Egyptian agenda. They were worthy of rest and freedom to live in ultimate allegiance to Yahweh, not Pharaoh. It was their God-given right. In *Sabbath as Resistance*, Walter Brueggemann notes, "The reason Miriam and the other women can sing and dance at the end of the exodus narrative is the emergence of a new social reality in which the life of the Israelite economy is no longer determined and compelled by the insatiable production quotas of Egypt and its gods."[1] Miriam longed for a new way of existing alongside her people; they would have the freedom to rest, and that was a form of nonviolent resistance. Scholar Phyllis Trible calls this approach "Miramic leadership," the embodied behavior of the first female prophet who unashamedly resisted a gross abuse of power at the Nile's bank and in her seaside song.[2] She's the first to distinguish the prophetic power of Israel from Egypt's abusive exploitation, setting aside power-motivated violence for freedom-focused nonviolence.[3] Miriam wasn't playing by another's rule book. It was her compassion and conviction that informed her choices.

For more than four hundred years, Israel had buckled under Egypt's unfair working conditions, grueling hours, and lack of care for human life. With no union or labor rights to cling to, the people had only their God, a trio of siblings to lead them, and an organized effort backed by plagues forcing their oppressors to see their lives as more than a means to an economic end. Spiritual formation writer Ruth Haley Barton explains, "As slaves in Egypt, the people of Israel were always at the mercy of the demands and expectations of a relentlessly consumeristic and opportunistic ruler who cared nothing for their well-being. But now . . . now that they had been freed from their bondage, they were being guided into a way of life that *worked for them*, by a God who knew them and loved them and only wanted to give them the very best."[4] Miriam's actions show that the way of rest isn't an elusive idea reserved for the well-resourced but rather a practice intended for all no matter where we've come from, what we've lost, or what we've achieved. The pharaohs of our day look different, but they still crave our time, attention, money, ideas, strength, and labor, leaving us stripped of sanity.

Even worse, we buy into the cultural conditioning that rest is indulgent and a way to reward ourselves, as if it's some carrot dangled on a string for the hardest working among us, always just out of reach. Nap Ministry founder Tricia Hersey claims, "Our drive and obsession to always be in a state of 'productivity' leads us to the path of exhaustion, guilt, and shame. We falsely believe we are not doing enough and that we must always be guiding our lives toward more. The distinction that must be repeated as many times as necessary is this: We are not resting to be productive. We are resting simply because it is our divine right to do so."[5] To hustle at the expense of rest is to make our way back to Egypt. Miriam knew this to be true. She was an advocate with the Divine to walk a new way free from oppressive rule, from impossible expectations that left her empty. Like Mother Miriam, we can choose to rest too.

Interestingly, rabbinic tradition suggests that Miriam was the Israelites' source of water and that she possessed a miraculous inner well that offered refreshment on their wilderness trek.[6] After her death in Kadesh, the wanderers went without water until Moses struck the rock (Num. 20:11). Throughout her life, her prophetic and confident nature carried an almost mystical meaning, and her identity was synonymous with refreshment to the people of Israel long before they reached the promised land. Like Miriam, we understand the practice of rest doesn't grant a stress-free existence; rather, it acknowledges our limitations, our finite nature, and our own wilderness wandering. Yet it still beckons us to tap out and quiet our souls, enabling us to see ourselves outside our commitments or achievements. Free of any cultural conditions, in rest we offer space for our minds, bodies, and souls to simply be.

As we walk the way of rest, may we heed the words of Jesus in Matthew 11:28–30:

> Come to me, all of you who are weary and carry heavy burdens, and I will give you rest. Take my yoke upon you. Let me teach you, because I am humble and gentle at heart, and you will find rest for your souls. For my yoke is easy to bear, and the burden I give you is light. (NLT)

PRAYER

God of Miriam,
I will advocate for rhythms of rest.
God of Israel's Daughters,
may my rest invite others to cherish theirs.

• • •

DECLARATION

I will rest no matter what today or tomorrow holds.
I will rest because it is my divine right.

• • •

QUESTIONS TO PONDER

- What does rest look like in this season?
- How does rest shape your view of yourself and others? Of the Divine?

10

Lionhearted Liturgies

> May your Kingdom come soon.
> May your will be done on earth,
>   as it is in heaven.
>
> —Matthew 6:10 (NLT)

Every emotion, from fear to love, anger to joy, is welcome in prayer, as evidenced in the Psalms. But what if we are at a loss for words? What if we are having trouble naming our desires? Our affliction? What if the intimacy of prayer feels inaccessible?

For generations, followers of Jesus have turned to liturgical prayers to give voice to their sorrow and peace, heartache and victory. Liturgical prayers are written for use in corporate or personal devotion and are often recited in accordance with the church calendar. Prayers from past saints echo through our mouths in an effort to connect with the Divine. Somehow, what's old is fresh, and prayers penned hundreds of years ago offer a vernacular that pinpoints our desires and desperate pleas in our modern day.

For Fannie Lou Hamer, liturgical prayers became her North Star, her connection to the Divine in times of trouble.

After Fannie Lou endured a violent, racially motivated attack within the confines of a jail cell, she called out to her Creator, her body wounded but her soul aflame. With strained breath, vision loss, and kidney damage, she sang of Paul and Silas's freedom from jail in Acts 16: "Paul and Silas began to shout, let my people go. Jail doors open and they walked out, let my people go."[1] Cellmates joined in as Fannie Lou sang out her melodious prayer, a liturgy for frightening moments behind bars. Fannie Lou sang her prayers in civil rights meetings, during church, and at protests as well. Her lionhearted liturgies spoke of the already-here-and-not-yet kingdom.

On a sticky August day in 1962, she and seventeen others went to register to vote at a Mississippi courthouse. On paper, women had been eligible to vote since the historic passage of the Nineteenth Amendment in 1920, but for Black women like Fannie Lou, barriers were put in place to keep them from participating in the political system. After being denied registration due to an unfair literacy exam, she returned home singing "This Little Light of Mine." She was then fired from her job for *attempting* to register. Jobless and healing from a "Mississippi appendectomy"—a hysterectomy performed without consent in order to curb the Black population—Fannie Lou was unflinching in her efforts to cast a ballot. Nearly a year later, in 1963, she completed voter registration in Charleston, South Carolina, but on her return trip to Mississippi she was arrested and later beaten in jail.[2]

Underneath it all, Fannie Lou's public work was fueled by her sturdy spiritual formation, as evidenced by her liturgies, her remixed prayers, Scripture woven with African American spirituals, and well-known hymns. Together, these formed her resistance liturgies, and they reflected the oppressive struggles of her community and their hope for social hierarchies to be turned upside down. Fannie Lou's rendition of "Go Tell It on the Mountain" adjusted the lyrics from "Go tell it on the mountain / that Jesus Christ is born" to "Go tell it on the mountain / to let my people go."[3] Fannie Lou learned to call on the Divine Liberator from her mama. Lou Ella Townsend sang while she picked cotton, "Oh, Lord, you know just how I feel. . . . Oh, Lord, they say you'd answer prayer. . . . Oh, Lord, I'm comin' to you again. . . . Oh, Lord, we sure do need you now."[4] Songs of freedom poured from her mother's mouth and into Fannie Lou's soul, bolstering her own belief in the God of Miriam and Mary, the one who partners with us for our freedom journey.

Fannie Lou's liturgies went far beyond her private practice of communion with the Divine. Breanna Barber notes, "Hamer's leadership utilized acts of public prayer through both a pastoral style—sung prayer used to comfort and strengthen her community—and a prophetic style—spoken prayer used to convey what she believed was God's will for America and to disrupt the established white social order."[5] Fannie Lou's Delta blues and Baptist roots gave way to fresh liturgy for a moment in history desperate for a voice like hers.[6]

Like Fannie Lou, we can name our desires and desperate pleas through borrowed prayers and weave in our hope for what might be. Liturgical prayers stretch us as we imagine a new way of being, of existing amid life's challenges. They aren't magic; rather, they are simply prayers that remind us we aren't the first ones to feel alone or afraid. We are interconnected with others, longing for the peace and liberty Christ offers. Borrowed phrases become a source of comfort and vision when we feel tired or rudderless.

In her book *To Light Their Way*, Kayla Craig writes, "Liturgy, the prayers of worship at times of celebration and lament, roots us in the ancient truth that God dwells in us and beside us. That we are called beloved and our children are called beloved, and that we are each a pebble in an ocean of deep, abiding love. Liturgy anchors us as the waves of real life wash over us. We pray in the mundane; we pray in the unknown; we pray when we have nothing left to give."[7] Our liturgies beckon the active engagement of the Creator. Fannie Lou knew this. Her mama did too. Fannie Lou Hamer, this sharecropper who left school at age twelve, who was beaten within an inch of her life, who knew her liturgies and her prayers, invited everyone who could hear to imagine a new reality. May we go and do likewise.

PRAYER

God of Fannie Lou,
help me to let my light shine and never be hidden.
God of Lou Ella,
I'm coming to you, and I sure do need you now.

DECLARATION

I will overcome, for my God is by my side.
We shall overcome as we partner with the Divine.

• • •

QUESTIONS TO PONDER

- What could a liturgy, a practice of prayer, look like for you in this season?
- Who can you encourage with your prayers?

11

Get in Formation

NIKOLE LIM

> "Certainly I will go with you," said Deborah. "But because of the course you are taking, the honor will not be yours, for the LORD will deliver Sisera into the hands of a woman."
>
> —Judges 4:9

The title of this chapter might have you thinking of Beyoncé's "Formation," and that song, off the 2016 album *Lemonade*, is more than a dope track. Spotlighting the disproportionate effects of Hurricane Katrina on Black communities and the senseless deaths of Trayvon Martin and other unarmed Black men, the "Formation" music video directly confronts systems of anti-Blackness, police brutality, and sexism.

From twerking in autocratic colonial attire at a Southern plantation to doing synchronized dancing in a swimming pool, Beyoncé asserts her feminine authority in places where Black women have been historically banned. Her lyrical mastery and unapologetic stance create an anthem of resistance. For many of us, she is a contemporary icon of a woman who understands and claims her decision-making authority.

Likewise, Deborah's position as a judge, prophet, and warrior daringly upended gender expectations of her day. In Judges 4, we learn of Deborah, a prophet presiding over Israel as a judge: a prominent position that gave her both religious and civil authority. The only female judge mentioned in the Bible, Deborah similarly subverts systems of sexist oppression.

After twenty years of oppression under the rule of the Canaanites, the Israelites looked to Deborah for a vision in which they could finally see their liberation. Her leadership gave them the opportunity to resist; she was the woman they'd been waiting for. Though the warriors of Israel lacked the courage to gather, rise up, and fight their enemy, Deborah was unwavering in living out her vision of liberation.

Armed with ten thousand warriors behind her and a clear vision from God, Deborah assumed her position of authority to fight for her people's liberation. Under Deborah's leadership, the Israelites won the war and slew the opposing troops, but Sisera, the enemy commander, slipped away.

Just as Deborah prophesied, the battle was won not by the male warriors of Israel but by another woman, Jael, who was potentially from a different cultural background. After Sisera fled the battlefield to seek refuge, Jael drove a tent peg into his head while he slept. Deborah and Jael moved in formation with God's will to win this battle and liberate the Israelites. As a result, the land had peace for forty years, passing a liberated existence to the next generation.

Rising up in a courageous battle against the enemies of oppression, sexism, and other forms of injustice requires an informed response. "Formation" is a play on words, where getting "in formation" also requires that we get *information* from our community about their needs, struggles, and hopes for the future.[1]

Deborah got informed about the challenges the Israelites were facing. Her court was held not in the city walls where male judges presided but under the shade of a honey tree. She communed with the people, administering justice in a space that was open, accessible, and inclusive—without walls, borders, or boundaries.

As community leaders, we must be open to listening, learning, and aligning with others around us, especially those whose rights have been violated. In learning from the wisdom of our community, we become better informed to promote justice, encourage unity, and fight for equity. By listening to the stories of others, we develop empathy, compassion, and a mutual understanding that the fight for justice is not me against you but *we* against the larger system of patriarchal, sexist, and religious empires.

While Deborah's and Jael's courageous acts liberated Israel, I'm not at all suggesting we suit up for war to annihilate our oppressors or drive tent pegs into the heads of unjust leaders. Instead, we can channel our visionary artistry, courage, and intelligence to offer an alternative to poverty, oppression, sexism, racism, homophobia, classism, and ableism. We must set aside all the ways we assert ourselves as better than other people. We must fight for a collective *we*, where all moving parts are moving to reconcile the brokenness among us.

So instead of fighting wars with violence, how can we embody the spirit of Deborah and get in formation?

We can start by finding the courage to stand up against oppression. Though Deborah was the only woman of her caliber (as recorded in the Bible), she took her rightful place as an authority figure ordained by God. The Lord was on Deborah's side as the Lord was also on the Israelites' side.

We can form alliances with women of diverse socio-economic and cultural backgrounds. Getting in formation requires us to stand side by side with each other in a common cause, a common battle. Just as Deborah and Jael aligned in a common goal of liberation.

We can uplift the power of Black women and other marginalized peoples. Deborah and Jael are celebrated as women who upheld the mantle for the ethnic (Israel) and gendered (women) underdogs of their time. We can too.

Let's courageously take up positions of power to bring liberation to others.

Let's form alliances with one another to fight against the powers that oppress us.

Let's see justice come about through our hands as women.

This battle is calling forth women to reclaim our divine right to slay.

PRAYER

God of Deborah and Jael,
grant me the courage to stand
up against oppression,
to stand in formation with others at the margins,
to move closer to the divine vision you've given me.
Allow me to listen and learn,
to practice empathy and compassion,
to sit among my community, fighting
for justice and equity.

. . .

DECLARATION

I will walk in my divine authority.
I will claim the divine source of power.
I will share my power and uplift others.

. . .

QUESTIONS TO PONDER

- What is God calling you to?
- What are systemic barriers that you need the courage to break through?
- Who are the marginalized around you that you can learn from?
- How can you stand in formation with other women in this pursuit of equity, justice, and power sharing?

12

Crafting Conditions of Care

"Shall I go and get one of the Hebrew women to nurse the baby for you?"

"Yes, go," she answered. So the girl went and got the baby's mother. Pharaoh's daughter said to her, "Take this baby and nurse him for me, and I will pay you." So the woman took the baby and nursed him. When the child grew older, she took him to Pharaoh's daughter and he became her son. She named him Moses, saying, "I drew him out of the water."

—Exodus 2:7–10

As a spiritual practice, crafting conditions of care that lead to renewal stretches beyond fellowship with other believers, forgiving those who've harmed us, or daily Scripture reading. These are all irrefutably valuable practices, but if we hope to offer formation and liberation for the flourishing of all image bearers, we must harness our brilliance and leverage our resources.

Moses's biological and adoptive mothers knew this to be true. In Exodus 2, we read of their combined efforts to craft conditions for young Moses to thrive amid the threat of infanticide. Moses's biological mother, Jochebed, created an environment where she could hide her son for months without getting caught by Pharaoh's henchmen. After only ninety days with her newborn baby—ninety days of nursing, naps on her chest, and prayers of protection—she fashioned a riverboat out of papyrus leaves and pitch, a water buggy she settled among the bulrushes with her precious baby inside. Perhaps she knew exactly how it would play out, that Pharaoh's daughter would look after her son. Or maybe it was a long shot, a hope that would in turn pay off. Either way, her plan worked. She turned a hopeless situation into a win-win for everyone, ensuring her son would live to see another day—protected by the very house that had vowed to destroy him and other Hebrew sons.

Pharaoh's daughter, the Midrash calls her Bithiah, spotted the basket among the reeds of the Nile and heard infant cries. She sent a maid to fetch it. On pulling the baby from the basket, she immediately took it upon herself to care for Moses, knowing full well he was among the hunted Hebrew baby boys. At Miriam's offer, she hired Jochebed as his wet nurse, to care for him until he was weaned. The biological mother and adoptive mother agreed on terms and conditions, collaborating to protect an innocent child from harm. After some time, Moses returned to his adopted mother once again. In *Defiant*, Kelley Nikondeha remarks, "Bithiah's care created an avenue of blessing that would serve him well into his adulthood, contributing to his liberative trajectory before he even fully embodied it."[1] Pharaoh's daughter's efforts to devise a caring space for Moses set the stage for a nation's deliverance, right under the nose of their chief oppressor.

From Jochebed and Bithiah's plans, we discover that crafting conditions of care requires proactive, more than reactive, ingenuity. Conviction coupled with action provided the conditions necessary for Moses to grow in a safe space.

Another group of women in history, like Moses's family, created an environment for a confederacy of nations to flourish. Long before Europe colonized the Americas, the Haudenosaunee (Iroquois) women crafted conditions that brought economic independence, bodily autonomy, national security, and mutual flourishing.

Tribal women were known to negotiate terms of war and peace, doing their darndest to prevent war and spare their sons' lives, echoing the hopes of mothers like Jochebed and Bithiah. Honoring shared knowledge, they sought to make wise agricultural decisions related to food supply and distribution, thus controlling their economy. Their social order of gender balance is considered by some authorities to be the world's oldest continuing democracy,[2] constructed with mutual flourishing in mind. What the Haudenosaunee women did out in the open—crafting conditions of care, protection, and preservation for their loved ones—Moses's mothers did in private.

Abuse and murder were rare among the Haudenosaunee, and violence against women and children was nearly unheard of. If any man abused his power or failed to uphold the egalitarian way, he'd face the music of the matriarchs. Suffragette leader Matilda Gage wrote of the Haudenosaunee Confederacy, "Never was justice more perfect; never was civilization higher."[3] Tribal women didn't benefit at the expense of others; instead, they valued the safety and well-being of every image bearer.

Like the Haudenosaunee women and Moses's mothers, we can practice crafting conditions—in small and big ways—that ensure intentional care and concern for those in our world, refusing to shore up advantages for ourselves at others' expense. By honoring the needs of others while not denying the needs of the self, we labor for a better tomorrow and honor the *imago Dei* in every living person. As we craft conditions for the flourishing of all, we make the invisible visible, the unseen seen. Honoring others leads to liberation from unfair laws and practices, advocates for freedom in warring nations, and provides resources for ignored populations. As we shepherd and lead, establish boundaries, negotiate and deliberate, vote and protest, plant and harvest, flourishing becomes commonplace.

PRAYER

God of Jochebed,
allow me to craft conditions of
care amid trying times.
God of Bithiah,
guide me as I leverage my resources for
the flourishing of all image bearers.
God of the Haudenosaunee Women,
grant me wisdom as I contribute to
a world in need of restoration.

DECLARATION

I will cultivate conditions of care
for those in my world.
I will contribute to systems of restorative freedom.

. . .

QUESTIONS TO PONDER

- What could it look like to craft conditions of care in your context?
- What does it mean for you to be selfless while not denying the needs of the self?

13

Lament to Heal

Teach your daughters how to wail; teach one another a lament.

—Jeremiah 9:20

Try as we might, we cannot skip over grief, ignore its presence, and hope we will escape unscathed. Life is too dastardly difficult. Too harsh to assume we'll get off scot-free.

Although loss is wounding, our best option is to voice our grief, honor our pain, and refuse to move on until we properly lament. Only then will we heal.

The wailing women lead the way.

In ancient times, guttural grief pierced every soul within earshot as these women's wails cut between heaven and earth. They flailed their arms, threw dust on their heads, disheveled their hair, and even bared their breasts as they wept. Their cries were not in vain; they had a message to deliver. These women were instructors, midwives of mourning, tasked with modeling lament. Charged with communal grief work, wailing women of the ancient world publicly proclaimed that all was not well with their souls. Intimate knowledge of deep sorrow and sadness qualified older women to wail, but in Jeremiah 9, *all* of Israel's daughters are beckoned to lead their community as they publicly grappled with grief, not as exhibitionists but as practitioners. In an ancient world where women held little institutional power, we witness a call for them to lead their community in the face of calamity.

Invaded by the Babylonians in 597 BCE and again ten years later, Jerusalem and the towns of Judah endured deadly devastation; not a soul was spared as their captors ruthlessly demolished everything precious to them. Pulling no punches, Jeremiah prophesied a bleak picture at the hands of Babylon for those who turned their backs on the Divine, but within his grim account, he called on the women to wail, to grieve, moving women from a place of social invisibility to a platform of authority and importance in a time of national crisis.[1] He asked not only for the skilled women to wail but for the wailing women to teach their daughters to wail as well, thus calling on half their population to publicize this national trauma. Jeremiah 9:17–21 records the prophet's instructions:

> This is what the LORD Almighty says:
>
> "Consider now! Call for the wailing women
>   to come;
>   send for the most skillful of them.
> Let them come quickly
>   and wail over us

till our eyes overflow with tears
    and water streams from our eyelids.
The sound of wailing is heard from Zion:
    'How ruined we are!
    How great is our shame!
We must leave our land
    because our houses are in ruins.'"

Now, you women, hear the word of the Lord;
    open your ears to the words of his mouth.
Teach your daughters how to wail;
    teach one another a lament.
Death has climbed in through our windows
    and has entered our fortresses;
it has removed the children from the streets
    and the young men from the public squares.

Their defeat was inevitable after Judah had opportunity after opportunity to right their wrongs but failed to do so. Rather than sulk in sorrow, they were invited to publicly proclaim their grief. To name the trauma that broke through their emotional, mental, and psychological defenses. To embody their loss through wails and whimpers as a holy response to their tragedy.

The wailing women of ancient times were skilled, likely trained in the art of public lament by older generations of wise women who taught them to express their pain within solemn rituals that moved stress through the body.[2] Familiar with loss and violence, poverty and subjugation, the wailing women were rich in the tradition of lament as both recipients and conduits, knowledgeable about which lamentation would suit an occasion. L. Juliana Claassens notes, "By means of creative actualization of the lament tradition, wailing women vocalized what people would have said or ought to have said—their laments truly represented a community response to trauma."[3] Their active role in grief work helped individuals to vocalize their trauma in the context of community rather than suffer alone. Their embodied response gave everyone permission to acknowledge their pain rather than suppress it. Like the wailing women of Jeremiah's time, in our lament we attend to our trauma, and we look for a new way forward.

Like their ancient mothers before them, weary women in Cameroon wailed for their losses: children murdered, neighbors kidnapped, and villages burned to the ground. The Anglophone Crisis between Northwest and Southwest Cameroon had left communities in the crossfire of armed separatists and national security forces. School shootings, sexual violence, bombings with improvised explosives, and extrajudicial killings were commonplace,[4] leaving over seven hundred thousand people, mostly women and girls, displaced since the crisis began in 2017.[5] Women in Cameroon have had little sway in the halls of power and fare far worse than men in times of war, but they did what women have done for centuries to grieve and plead for a better way: they participated in communal lament.

In May 2019, on the prime minister's arrival in Bamenda, Cameroon, scores of women wailed for peace when he visited the conflict-torn region. The wailing women, from varied cultural groups throughout the country, purposely amplified their distress as a means to move peace talks forward.[6] One woman shared, "These are the women of the North-West region who have been in pain for the past three years, and because we heard that the prime minister is coming here today we decided that we should come out and cry aloud because the flow of blood has been too much. There is pain! We don't sleep! There are incessant killings every day. We think that as women we have to do our part of the job by coming out to cry, to tell the powers that be that they should try to put an end to this."[7] Cameroonian women and their daughters suffered tremendously in their quest to access basic resources amid the conflict, and although they hadn't been able to claim bodily autonomy or safety, they could wail, acknowledge their sorrow, and bear witness to their communal grief in hopes of a better tomorrow.

Our cries of lament are necessary for us to mourn all that we've lost, all that's been taken from us. Naming what has happened is vital to the healing process. Not a step to skip but a ritual to embrace, lament clarifies our limitations and our finitude. Lament contends with untamed grief. As we accept the sting of suffering, our grief becomes the seedbed for our healing, our strength. When we extend beyond an individual process to a communal calling, we open the doors for our brothers and sisters, our sons and daughters, to thread their cries together and vocalize their anguish too.

We may be tempted to gloss over our wounds with platitudes when wails are what's truly needed. Our bodies hold our traumas, abuses, and shame, and as embodied creatures, we are not weak when we wail; rather, it's in our cries of vulnerability that our strength is developed. Honestly, few of us have made it far in life unscathed; most of us bear scars that we wouldn't wish on our worst enemy. Yet it is the women who've spoken of the bitterness of life, the women who've named their losses and openly lamented their suffering, who have led us in times of tragedy. They're the women we've been waiting for, the women we wail with. The women we're becoming.

PRAYER

God of the Wailing Women,
help me to name my pain and grieve it well.
God of Our Cameroonian Sisters,
may my cries make way for peace.

• • •

DECLARATION

I will embrace the ritual of lament,
to heal my body, mind, and soul.

• • •

QUESTIONS TO PONDER

- What can lament look like, or sound like, for you in this season?
- How has unnamed and untamed grief affected your healing journey?

14

A Culture of Belonging

LUCRETIA CARTER BERRY

If one part suffers, every part suffers with it; if one part is honored, every part rejoices with it.

—1 Corinthians 12:26

Belonging is a fundamental human need. It encompasses a sense of identity and security, offering a sense of home and acceptance. We all desire to join a community or a society where we are accepted, valued, and connected. In a culture of belonging, we are welcomed, respected, and appreciated; we thrive.

Septima Poinsette Clark's pivotal contributions to civil rights began with her thirst for knowledge. Septima was born in 1898 in Charleston, South Carolina, into a community that was designed to exclude her from getting a quality education. She was unwilling to accept the status quo, however, saying, "I believe unconditionally in the ability of people to respond when they are told the truth. We need to be taught to study rather than to believe, to inquire rather than to affirm."[1]

Septima saw education as a pathway to empowerment and believed that knowledge could serve as a powerful tool for challenging racial inequality and advancing civil rights, so she dreamed of becoming a teacher. Septima also dreamed of a future where Black citizens would have equal rights and opportunities, an America where they would belong.

Septima's father was a former slave, and her mother worked as a laundress. They lived in conditions of economic hardship, and Septima needed to work and contribute to her family's income. She had to balance her studies with working as a domestic servant to help support her family. Racial discrimination permeated every aspect of daily life in the Jim Crow South. Segregation laws dictated where Black Americans could eat, shop, and travel, further marginalizing them and reinforcing White supremacy.

After teaching in South Carolina, Septima joined the Highlander Folk School in Tennessee, an institution focused on empowering marginalized communities through education that proved to be a training ground for activists such as Rosa Parks, Martin Luther King Jr., Ella Baker, Anne Braden, and Zilphia Horton. Septima, now an educator and inspired by her experiences there, utilized its principles in the development of Citizenship Schools, which empowered Black Americans to become active participants in the democratic process and to challenge voter suppression and racial segregation along the way. Without a doubt, in her professional and civic life, she lived and led in a way that invited everyone to belong.

The Citizenship Schools had a profound impact on the civil rights movement, as Black voters in the South played a pivotal role in dismantling segregation. Septima's work laid the foundation for significant milestones, such as the Civil Rights Act of 1964 and the Voting Rights Act of 1965, both of which marked real strides toward helping to transform the soul of our nation.[2]

Like Septima, many of us know that feeling of estrangement—of being written out of consciousness, systematically excluded, banished from the human family—our likeness demonized and vilified to justify our exclusion and exploitation. Rules are conjured and weaponized to legalize and normalize alienation. Gatekeepers invested in retaining power inhumanely contort themselves to be inhospitable to those they have deemed "other": the citizen who is not male, White, and wealthy; the church member whose faith perspective doesn't fit in the box shaped by the leaders; or the person whose gender identity transcends a binary worldview.

Though we've suffered alienation and degradation, we break their spell when we push for belonging. We reach deep beyond the pattern of power hoarding and identity policing. We tap into our divine design to cultivate a space of welcome. In Acts 17:28, we are reminded of the profound truth that in God we find our very being and existence. The Scripture proclaims, "For in him we live and move and have our being," emphasizing the intimate connection between our lives and the Divine. We are lovingly referred to as God's "offspring," signifying that we are all part of a greater family, universally belonging to God and each other. Ultimately, our very beginning, our essence, is in belonging.

Even when robbed of dignity, respect, and rights, we make our way home where we live, where we move, and where we *belong*: in God. Power-hoarding, identity-contorting gatekeepers, try as they might, cannot rip God's reflection from us. They can teach propaganda. They can legalize obstacles. But they can't overwrite or destroy God's imprint. We bear God's own image of belonging. Systemic oppression, degradation, and alienation set the stage for us to elevate belonging as our response. We simply can't help it!

Belonging is a unifying bond that transcends imposed distinctions: "There is neither Jew nor Gentile, neither slave nor free, nor is there male and female, for you are all one in Christ Jesus" (Gal. 3:28). Though unique, we are woven together in the tapestry of God's love. Belonging binds us to one another. Therefore, "If one part suffers, every part suffers with it; if one part is honored, every part rejoices with it" (1 Cor. 12:26). Our belonging to each other compels us to extend empathy, compassion, and support, to foster a community where everyone can thrive.

In belonging, we're seen, safe, and satisfied. We're stretched to be our fullest selves in Christ—shaped and forged into the likeness of love and peace. This is not to be confused with looking for approval, which is conditional on obedience or contorted by the need to conform. Rather, belonging invites others to fully know us and others to be fully known, just as Christ models.

May we become women of belonging, like Septima and others in her stead.

PRAYER

Most High,
in a world marked by exclusion and alienation,
I will seek solace and togetherness.
God of Belonging,
strengthen our bonds of empathy,
compassion, and support for one another.
In you, we find our true home, where all are
welcomed and loved unconditionally.

• • •

DECLARATION

We know the feeling of being marginalized,
our identities nullified by oppressive systems.
Yet we find comfort in your promise that in
you, we live, move, and have our being.
You lovingly call us your offspring, signifying
that we are all part of a greater family,
universally belonging to you and each other.

• • •

QUESTIONS TO PONDER

- How can you actively contribute to fostering a culture of belonging in your own life?
- How can you actively contribute to promoting inclusiveness in the lives of those around you?

15

Your Beautiful Body

God created human beings;
   he created them godlike,
reflecting God's nature.
   He created them male and female.

—Genesis 1:27 (Message)

In times of scandal, women are often blamed for how they carried themselves, what they wore or didn't wear, and how they moved through the world in their bodies. Somehow, society has accepted that if something has gone wrong, it must have been the woman who started it.

Unsure if that's the case? One need only look to Eve to confirm any suspicions.

An eternal soul enfleshed, Mother Eve walked naked and unashamed among the bluebirds and wildflowers of the garden of Eden. As the first woman to walk the earth, she was crafted by the Creator as good, every inch of her deemed wonderful. Her thighs, her hips, her arms, her lips, all of it majestic. She would be the first among us to feel the earth under her feet, the hot sun warm her cheeks, and the wind blow through her hair. She was the first of us to feel exuberant joy and furious anger, deep sadness and debilitating worry. As the mother of all, she was more than a helper, more than a body to bear children, and she deserves to be remembered for more than the downfall of humanity.

Throughout the centuries, many paintings have depicted Eve as a woman embodying unbridled desire, shame, and sin, but objectification is in the eye of the beholder: physical, sexual, and theological. Paraded around for millennia as justification to subjugate women's bodies, Mother Eve has been painted as a temptress—a corrupt woman who deserved punishment. As the narrative often goes, women, daughters of Mother Eve, are impressionable and prone to deviance, and they require control by the men in their world. Even worse, women are looking for opportunities to lead men astray, far from their values and their God. Women may employ charm and the curves of their bodies to get their way with men as Eve did with Adam, inviting him into sin. Eve couldn't be trusted, and neither can her daughters.

Women's bodies have been viewed as property, as objects. Monastic fathers infused their faith with Greek philosophy that correlated women's bodies with the flesh and men with the spirit. Aristotle held to the belief that women were biologically and psychologically inferior.[1] Christian apologist Tertullian believed of women, "You are the devil's gateway. . . . How easily you destroyed man, the image of God. Because of the death which you brought upon us, even the Son of God had to die."[2] The idea that a woman's body is inherently corrupt has woven its way through both purity culture *and* rape culture, as both treat women's bodies as objects to be controlled and to be blamed for men's actions. Sadly, the intersection of gender and race has exacerbated this toxic thinking, painting women of color as hypersexual, with harm against their bodies happening at higher rates than those of White women.[3] Yet in the garden, the first woman wasn't created to be labeled by any such harmful stereotypes: she was created as a reflection of the Divine. We all are.

Mother Eve hasn't been given the opportunity to be seen as the woman we've been waiting for. Yet that's literally what she was. She wasn't a cure for Adam's loneliness but rather was created to co-reign alongside him, representing what would be half the population for all time. Not an object to be ruled, sold, harmed, or exploited (or even a beauty to pursue), she's an expression of the Creator's imagination who herself can create life. A patriarchal reading of Genesis 3:16 presumes men must control women since the Creator dictated to Eve that "[your husband] will rule over you." But scholar Philip B. Payne explains that Genesis 3:16 is "God's statement of what will result from the fall, not God's decree of what should be. Like every other result of the fall, this is something new, not in the original creation. It is a distortion of God's design." Payne continues, "Since man's ruling over a woman—even good rule—is a result of the fall, man must not have ruled over woman before the fall. Furthermore, Christ, the promised seed of the woman, has overcome the fall (Gen. 3:15; 1 Cor. 15:45).

New creatures freed by Christ should not foster any of the tragic consequences the fall introduced, including man's rule over woman."[4] It wasn't condemnation and control of all women tucked in Eve's rebuke but the coming of grace for a woman who got it wrong. Her redemption was already in motion. Not only was she the first woman among us but also the very first to vulnerably sit before the Divine and face her shame.

In contrast, Mother Mary has been praised throughout history for offering her body in partnership with the Divine to birth Jesus. Painted as the Madonna for centuries and hailed as the woman we can look up to at the *expense* of Eve, Mother Mary is the one we should applaud, not her predecessor. Irenaeus of Lyons advanced the notion that young Mary is the new Eve. Irenaeus claimed, "Adam had to be recapitulated in Christ, so that death might be swallowed up in immortality, and Eve in Mary, so that the Virgin, having become another virgin's advocate, might destroy and abolish one virgin's disobedience by the obedience of another virgin."[5] According to Irenaeus, the two woman embodied differing morals, one associated with our communal death and the other our communal resurrection. The contrast was spelled out by the early church father St. Ephrem:

> Mary gave birth without having relations with a man. As in the beginning, Eve was born from Adam without a carnal relationship, so it happened for Joseph and Mary, his wife. Eve brought to the world the murdering Cain; Mary brought forth the Lifegiver. One brought into the world him who spilled the blood of his brother (cf. Gen. 4:10–16); the other, him whose blood was poured out for the sake of his brothers. One brought into the

world him who fled, trembling because of the curse of the earth; the other brought forth him who, having taken the curse upon himself, nailed it to the Cross.[6]

Not only did early church fathers and Renaissance artists paint Eve as a polarizing temptress, they argued their belief by co-opting Mary's choice to carry the Divine in her womb. Eve's embodied life is reduced to a story of what not to do. Author Hye Hyun Han shares, "The contrast between Eve and Mary and the objectification of women in Christianity based on this comparison are still operative. In terms of patriarchy, every Christian woman is trapped in a negative image of Eve rather than belonging to the ranks of perfect femininity as Mary does."[7]

When we paint our first mother as a woman who embodies the worst in us, we fail to see how precious she was, how beautiful her life was, and the faithfulness of her Creator. As we look upon the kindness and majesty of our Creator God, we'll find an artist who painted Eve as lovely, and every daughter after her, a beloved and treasured body worthy of honor and grace, safety and respect. As we embrace our bodies, may we reject any label ill-suited for a daughter of God, for we are created to co-reign and mend the earth.

PRAYER

God of Mother Eve,
lead me to embody goodness and grace.
Creator of My Body,
let me treasure my body, its strength and frailty.

DECLARATION

My hips, lips, thighs, and arms are
beautiful, I know this full well.
I will honor my body and the stories it carries.

· · ·

QUESTIONS TO PONDER

- In what ways have you been conditioned to judge a woman by how she carries herself?
- By what she wears?
- By what's happened to her?

16

Discernment

And this is my prayer: that your love may abound more and more in knowledge and depth of insight, so that you may be able to discern what is best and may be pure and blameless for the day of Christ, filled with the fruit of righteousness that comes through Jesus Christ—to the glory and praise of God.

—Philippians 1:9–11

Can you tell when something is not quite right? When an idea, decision, or teaching looks great on paper but not in practice? When ill intent is masked with platitudes, or when you've been gaslit into believing another's version of the truth?

To become the women we've been waiting for, we cannot forgo the practice of discernment for detecting and testing whether what is before us is right, true, beautiful, and good. More than elementary perception or cursory judgment, discernment is a gift of the Spirit to practice in all seasons. And its impact may stretch further than we could imagine.

In 2 Kings 22, King Josiah's advisers discover the Book of the Law (thought to be Deuteronomy) during repairs to the temple. Deeply grieved after accounts of Judah's rebellion against the ways of God are read to him, Josiah, the chief priest Hilkiah, and the royal court turn to Huldah, a prophetess, to discern the divine instruction of God for Judah. On her word, they accept the validity of the text and ask how they should proceed. Wisely, she prophesies of coming judgment but reveals that Josiah will be spared because he humbled himself before the Lord, tearing his robes and weeping in the Lord's presence. His response to listening to God's Word means he will not witness the coming disaster but will be buried in peace. All that she speaks of comes to pass.

Although other prophets could have counseled King Josiah, Huldah's contemporaries sought her out. Her wise assessments and reverence for the Divine were known and trustworthy in the eyes of the king and his priest. Upon her prophecy, King Josiah renews communal efforts to follow the Lord and hold Judah to their covenant agreement. Huldah's competence is rooted in her wise discernment, and it informed national decisions that ushered in renewal.

Another woman in the Old Testament who practiced discernment and saved her husband's life was Zipporah. In Exodus 4, as Moses is en route to Egypt to face off with Pharaoh, God is about to kill Moses for his disobedience when Zipporah wisely recognizes her husband's precarious situation, hastily circumcises their son, and touches the foreskin to Moses's feet. This vivid detail included in the exodus narrative speaks to Zipporah's knowledge of the Hebrew God and quick action in a high-stakes situation. At a moment when we might expect Moses to act decisively, it's his wife's wise discernment that saves his life and allows her to act as a mediator between God and her husband.

Another passage speaks to discernment developed over decades. Elderly and widowed Anna, mentioned in Luke 2:36–38, spent the majority of her life worshiping, fasting, and praying at the temple. When she catches a glimpse of young Jesus, she tells Joseph and Mary that their beloved son will one day redeem Jerusalem. Her intimate knowledge of the Divine personified was no doubt anchored in wisdom forged by prayer and fasting.

Henri Nouwen, in his book *Discernment*, writes, "Our God is a God who cares, heals, guides, directs, challenges, confronts, corrects. To discern means first of all to listen to God, to pay attention to God's active presence, and to obey God's prompting, direction, leadings, and guidance."[1] Nouwen infers that discernment will look different for each of us, just as it did for Huldah, Zipporah, and Anna, but it requires all of us to be attuned to the Divine and grow in the knowledge of how God works. As we mature, and moral, ethical, social, financial, and spiritual issues become more nuanced and complex, we find, as Charles Spurgeon is credited with explaining, that "discernment is not knowing the difference between right and wrong. It's knowing the difference between right and almost right."[2] It requires that we approach tender subjects, teachings, or situations with a critical eye, sharpened mind, and wise heart to determine what to accept or reject.

Discernment doesn't mimic the zeitgeist or popular opinion of one's in-group, nor does it assume that whoever is loudest is right. Romans 12:2 reads, "Don't become so well-adjusted to your culture that you fit into it without even thinking. Instead, fix your attention on God. You'll be changed from the inside out. Readily recognize what he wants from you, and quickly respond to it. Unlike the culture around you, always dragging you down to its level of immaturity, God brings the best out of you, develops well-formed maturity in you" (Message). May our practice of discernment be rooted in our connection to the Divine and understanding of the Scriptures so we can wisely navigate our days as we seek the fullness of Christ.

PRAYER

God of Huldah,
may I clearly heed your word and way.
God of Zipporah,
allow me to quickly discern situations with wisdom.
God of Anna,
grant me decades to worship you.

• • •

DECLARATION

I will let wisdom be my guide.
Grant within me a heart to discern what
is right, wrong, and almost right.

QUESTIONS TO PONDER

- Who models a healthy practice of discernment for you and how?
- What are questions you could ask, in any given situation, that would prompt a hunt for wisdom?

PART 3

THE
STORIES
THAT
FORM US

The ability to tell your own story, in words or
images, is already a victory, already a revolt.

—Rebecca Solnit

17

Gentleness

Let your gentleness be evident to all.

—Philippians 4:5

In an effort to protect ourselves from emotional and physical harm, we may shed gentleness and opt for judgment instead. Gentleness can feel impossible to embody in a world jaded by trauma and tragedy, slights and snubs. Judging others and withholding compassion can seem to offer a semblance of control, a form of twisted power, but gentleness insists we remain soft and tender to ourselves and to others—even if it seems that a tough approach to life will offer us more protection.

The invitation to practice gentleness is threaded throughout the New Testament. To give just a few examples:

Therefore, as God's chosen people, holy and dearly loved, clothe yourselves with compassion, kindness, humility, gentleness, and patience. (Col. 3:12)

Let your gentleness be evident to all. The Lord is near. (Phil. 4:5)

But in your hearts revere Christ as Lord. Always be prepared to give an answer to everyone who asks you to give the reason for the hope that you have. But do this with gentleness and respect. (1 Pet. 3:15)

If gentleness—a humanizing kindness gifted to others—is a practice to cultivate in our spiritual journey, we'd be wise to exercise it on ourselves in a world that seems happy to tell us all the ways we fail to measure up.

Judy Heumann, a legendary disability rights advocate, heard such messages from the time she was a child. After she contracted polio at eighteen months old, her doctor suggested institutionalizing her, a common practice at the time. Instead, Judy's parents, orphaned by the Holocaust and intimately aware of how unjust societies judge and treat the least among them, became her greatest advocates.

Due to Judy Heumann's confinement to a wheelchair, her mother was asked to remove her from her Brooklyn neighborhood school on her first day of kindergarten in the early 1950s on the premise that she posed a fire hazard. For years, her mother fought with the administration until they finally allowed Judy to join a basement classroom with other children with disabilities. Limited to drawing, napping, and doing worksheets in a windowless room, Judy and her class-mates found little was expected of them.

History repeated itself when as an adult Judy applied to teach in New York City and was refused a license because she couldn't walk.[1] With the support of her community, she sued the board of education in federal court and was heard by the formidable judge Constance Baker Motley, the first Black female federal judge in the United States. Awarded her teaching license after winning the lawsuit, Judy went on to teach at the neighborhood school that had denied her access to kindergarten. One obituary for Judy, who died in 2023, includes these lines: "She seemed to know in her bones that she deserved to be included. Disability is not an inherent tragedy or broken version of a whole life, but another form of human variation. Even as a child, she lived in a story of her own making, and she expected the world to bend to it, not the other way around. What kind of human comes into the world with that kind of audacity?"[2] I'll tell you what kind: one who knows she's loved; one who is gentle with herself, her story, and her body.

After leaving her teaching position, Judy cofounded several disability rights groups and advised the United Nations, World Bank, and sitting presidents on disability policy. After fighting ableist discrimination in education and employment systems that had no interest in treating her fairly, she made it her mission to enshrine disability rights for brothers and sisters with disabilities in the American legal landscape. She shared, "Disability only becomes a tragedy for me when society fails to provide the things we need to lead our lives—job opportunities or barrier-free buildings, for example. It is not a tragedy to me that I'm living in a wheelchair."[3] Judy encouraged those in power to refrain from imposing limits on how another is allowed to thrive, codifying gentleness without reservation, without qualifiers. For followers of Jesus, the practice of gentleness that the New Testament implores we pursue does not withhold compassion, care, or opportunity to flourish. Like Judy, we can recognize that the abstract quickly becomes concrete when it affects how others live, move, and operate.

In Scripture, Paul instructs the church in Philippi to let their gentleness be evident to *all*, and I suspect it's difficult to be gentle with others without first being gentle with ourselves. We must honor our limitations and believe without a shadow of a doubt that we are worthy of love, care, grace, and mercy—no matter how others perceive us or have treated us. Gentleness is a tall order if we've experienced neglect, abuse, or harm. Rejection rooted in our experiences clouds our ability to see ourselves as beloved, and to bandage our wounds we often pursue perfectionism, projecting shame-induced judgment on others after it's had its way with us. Therapist Jenny Palmiotto remarks, "Shame is the powerful leader. Judgment is her mouthpiece."[4] But as we're gentle with ourselves, granting ourselves compassion, we're inclined to be gentle with others without condition or agenda.

Judy was relentlessly gentle with herself in a time when others weren't. Her life and work hint at the idea that we mustn't crumble under the weight of perfectionism or judgment. She explained in *Ability* magazine, "My life was constricted not by my disability but by the stories others told themselves about what disabled people are capable of."[5] Judgment trumped gentleness and she suffered for it, but it didn't deter her. Like Judy, we must relentlessly practice gentleness toward ourselves and resist the temptation to judge. As gentleness lightens the burden of shame, we're molded into the woman we've been waiting for—a woman whose gentleness is evident to all.

PRAYER

God of Judy Heumann,
teach me to be relentlessly gentle with myself.
God of Constance Baker Motley,
grant me gentleness for the benefit of all.

• • •

DECLARATION

I will choose gentleness over judgment.
I will work to recognize the inherent worth of all.

• • •

QUESTIONS TO PONDER

- Have you failed to be gentle with yourself recently? Why?
- How can your gentleness be evident to all?

18

Reclaiming
What's Been Lost

Fools mock at reparation, but among the upright there
is favor.

—Proverbs 14:9 (NET)

What happens after we've been emotionally, socially,
or sexually robbed? Or what if we've been the one to
rob another? How do we right our wrongs? How do we
recover after our world has been ruptured? In our effort
to honor the self and push for social renewal, becoming
women of repair is imperative—not to mention messy,
nuanced, seemingly undignified at times, and perpetu-
ally insistent. A heart for repair implies that what has
happened to us, or to others, shouldn't have happened,
and we'll do our best to ensure it doesn't happen again.

But the act of repair, of reparations—repentance coupled with restitution—doesn't normally happen overnight. Sometimes, it takes generations.

The Sansei women know this to be true.

The day after the bombing of Pearl Harbor, the bank accounts of Japanese citizens were frozen, among them many first-generation Japanese immigrants (Issei) and second-generation Japanese Americans (Nisei). Months after Franklin D. Roosevelt signed Executive Order 9066, which stripped Japanese Americans of their constitutional rights, Issei women scrambled to hide or destroy their priceless family heirlooms—books written in Japanese and treasured family photographs— they feared could be considered contraband. Not long after, men and women of Japanese ancestry and their American-born children packed their lives into a single suitcase each as they were forcibly evacuated from their homes for internment in horse stables and fairgrounds across the West. The US government responded to Pearl Harbor with hysteria and suspicion. Subjugation was painted as patriotism.

Although interned women, most of them between fifteen and thirty years old, attempted to create private spaces in the camp using blankets or leftover building supplies, these measures didn't provide the safety they longed for. Nina Wallace reports that life in the camps robbed them of their dignity, "Women were often harassed, followed, threatened by White guards. At 'home,' instances of domestic violence and sexual abuse were often audible in neighboring barracks and became common knowledge around the camp."[1] To add insult to injury, reporting abuse led to public shame and isolation. Trapped and with no end in sight, these women saw that no one was coming to the rescue, so they rescued each other.

Stuck at the intersection of racism and sexism in the camps, Japanese women sought work to build a future—in food service, administration, and local hospitals. Others were able to pursue higher education outside the camp, gaining furlough long enough to attend classes and develop skills they could use back at the camp, such as teaching young ones, nursing each other to health, and writing for the camp newspapers to boost morale and build collective agency. They endured tyrannical circumstances yet found ways to reclaim agency for themselves, bucking Western *and* Eastern cultural norms that failed to value their personhood. Nisei women decried arranged marriages, and Issei mothers protested the draft of their sons with letter-writing campaigns to politicians in Washington.[2] Writing for *Breaking the Chains* magazine, Judy Cheng remarked, "They resisted the best way they knew how—creating support networks, and becoming self-reliant and independent."[3] When everything, both material and immaterial, was stolen from them, they became the women they desperately needed to be. But they deserved more than saving themselves. They deserved to reclaim what had been stolen and lost.

Six months after World War II ended, internment camps closed with zero redress and a one-way train ticket home for those unfairly incarcerated. Since family separation was common, it took many Japanese women a long time to finally locate their family members. Post-internment life issued a second wave of humiliation, with Japanese families returning home to find their houses looted, their businesses ransacked, their farms destroyed, and their reputation as worthy US citizens shattered. Executive Order 9066 led to $400 million in damages for those of Japanese ancestry in the United States and the generational trauma still felt today. All in the name of "national security." But the Sansei (third-generation Japanese Americans) women refused to let the story end there.

For four decades, the younger generation of Japanese women organized and fought for restitution and a formal apology from the US government for what happened to their mothers and fathers, grandmothers and grandfathers. Their efforts were acknowledged when President Ronald Reagan signed the Civil Liberties Act of 1988 into law, offering a formal apology on behalf of the US government for the wrongful imprisonment of more than 110,000 people whose only "crime" was being Japanese. This apology included a $20,000 payment for each of the sixty-five thousand surviving internees for breach of their constitutional rights. No longer willing to stomach humiliation, the Sansei rewrote the story to include repentance from the president and restitution from the nation's coffers. They fought for repair that was their due, and they succeeded in restoring dignity for their families.

Reclaiming what's been lost, or seeking reparations, demands we identify the emotional, spiritual, physical, financial, or sexual theft that stains our story. It begs us to name each experience, one by one, examine its impact, and seek for those wrongs to be made right. That may look like seeking restitution on a national level as the daughters and granddaughters of Japanese immigrants did, or it may look like healing from spiritual or sexual abuse—standing up to those who've harmed us or seeking sobriety for years lost to addiction—on our road to recovery.

As we seek to repair what's been lost or stolen in our own lives, that spirit of restoration extended to others is also an act of social healing. Historian Lee B. Spitzer notes, "Moving beyond stultifying guilt, the spiritual discipline of reparations embraces humility, repentance, caring, generosity, and self-sacrifice, in response to past social injustices and Jesus's articulation of the values of the kingdom of God. It represents a constructive way forward for serious disciples of Jesus to express genuine sorrow for peoples who have been harmed in the past and solidarity with those who presently are placed in difficult life situations because of past and continuing injustices."[4] Compassion with decisive action and participation will look different for each of us. A restorative mindset was famously modeled by Zacchaeus in Luke 19. The Jewish tax collector gave away half his money to the poor and vowed to repay those he'd swindled four times what he'd taken after he found acceptance with Jesus. While Jesus never demanded he make reparations, Zacchaeus likely would have been familiar with Leviticus 6:1–5, which offers a clear directive to the Hebrews to restore what's been stolen. On a grander scale, we're restored to right standing with God after the fall through Christ's death and resurrection, an act of repair for humanity for all time.

To reclaim what's been lost on behalf of ourselves and others is to follow the Divine and cowrite a new ending to the stories we inhabit. Duke Kwon and Greg Thompson sum up reparations this way: "The call of reparations is not merely for a check to be written or for a debt to be repaid but for a world to be repaired."[5]

As women, many of us are taught to be nice at the expense of being forthright—suffering through our losses, being seen rather than heard, hoping that what happened to others won't happen to us. But as we seek to build a just world for generations to come, we must stand and reclaim what's been lost *and* demand reparations, mending not only our individual stories but also our collective one.

PRAYER

God of Issei and Nisei Generations,
give me the courage to endure the unthinkable.
God of the Sansei Generation,
lead me to reclaim what's been lost and stolen.

•••

DECLARATION

I will gift bravery and endurance
to future generations.
I honor the endurance of past generations.

•••

QUESTIONS TO PONDER

- In your context, what wrongs can you seek to help make right?
- As you reflect on emotional, spiritual, physical, financial, or sexual theft, do you have any healing that you need to pursue in your own life or on behalf of others?

19

Befriending Grief

KEISHA POLONIO

When Jesus saw her weeping, and the Jews who had come along with her also weeping, he was deeply moved in spirit and troubled. "Where have you laid him?" he asked.

"Come and see, Lord," they replied.
Jesus wept.

—John 11:33–35

Grandmothers are always teaching us in the stories they tell. When they share the history of a cherished family recipe, they remind us of the importance of legacy. When they recount the details of their day, they reveal the importance of the mundane. When they tell us how things used to be, they invite us to remember what should not be forgotten. When we eat at our grandmothers' tables, lay our weary bodies on their couches, or sit at their feet as children, we witness the stories that shaped them.

Grandmother stories shaped Ella Jo Baker, a civil rights leader whose grandmother's accounts of enslavement became a catalyst for racial justice and social freedom efforts. Ella Jo was born in Norfolk, Virginia, in 1903, but she grew up on her grandmother's farm in North Carolina. This farm was formerly part of the plantation where Ella Jo's grandmother was enslaved. Ella Jo's bare feet would run free on ground that had been soaked with her ancestors' blood and tears. As she played in the fields, singing her favorite chorus to herself, her voice joined those of the many who came before her, chanting songs of freedom to get them through the day. On this land that had been tilled and reconciled, Ella Jo would sit and have her hair braided and her scalp greased while listening to stories of defiance. Ella Jo's grandmother never shied away from retelling the horrors that had happened to her. She shared stories of torture for resisting participation in an arranged marriage, fighting injustice in her own way.[1] Ella Jo's grandmother invited Ella Jo into her grief and sorrow.

Ella Jo leaned into complex spaces and held tension allowing for rage, silence, and tears. She listened to countless stories about racially motivated attacks, murders, and discrimination, and still she formulated strategies for moving forward. She listened intently, discerned profoundly, and noticed what others often overlooked.[2] Ella Jo served those in her community and acknowledged all they carried within their weary souls and burdened minds. She made room to see the fullness of a person. If you asked Ella Jo where she learned this profound ability to witness against injustice and push for equality, she would have told you that she learned it from her grandmother.

Ella Joe Baker was a quiet leader of the civil rights movement. She cared for the many and the few as she served as a director of branches of the National Association for the Advancement of Colored People (NAACP), curating educational programs to ensure Black Americans in the South could obtain leadership roles. She continued the fight against racial discrimination after the Montgomery bus boycott, when she became the first executive director of Martin Luther King Jr.'s Southern Christian Leadership Conference (SCLC). When Ella Jo heard about college students in Greensboro protesting segregation by sitting at a Woolworth's lunch counter, she met with the young activists. That meeting birthed the Student Nonviolent Coordinating Committee (SNCC), which she helped form as a space for emerging activists to find their voices.[3]

No matter what she did or what job title she held, Ella Jo knew that grief must be embraced because it's a part of who we are. The pain and losses of our lives long to be acknowledged and felt. When we allow ourselves to feel the emotions, the world is quick to judge our responses, but we must do so to heal. When we express the sorrow of our lives, we can take steps toward healing our spiritual, emotional, and cognitive wounds. Befriending grief is an invitation to restore our souls, and this soul work allows us to live fully embodied lives, aware of the joys and glimmers and shadows and pain. If we're present to ourselves, we're able to attune ourselves to the grief present in others.

Jesus was also deeply impacted by a story of grief. In John 11:33–35, we witness him weeping along with

Mary and the crowd gathered to mourn the death of his friend Lazarus. He felt it too. He was angry too. He cried too.

The unnamed grandmother of Ella Jo reminds us to make room for grief. She teaches us, by example, not to suppress our sorrow but to engage its complexities. Even in a world that hushes our suffering and tells us to silence our pain, she somehow knew "grief work is soul work."[4] This soul work offers profound freedom and healing.

We can carry on the legacy of Ella Jo Baker by sharing our grief and giving witness to the grief of others. We carry on the legacy of unnamed grandmothers by committing to the soul work of befriending grief and inviting others to join us.

PRAYER

God Who Sees,
help me to be a witness to my pain
and the pain of those around me.
Jesus Who Wept,
free my tears to wash over the losses I've endured.
Spirit That Fills,
come again and do what only you can.

• • •

DECLARATION

I will invite myself to slow down.
I will behold sorrow;
I will befriend grief.

QUESTIONS TO PONDER

- How might you better befriend grief?
- Why is it vital to invite others into your sorrow?

20

Her Story

But when the attendants delivered the king's command, Queen Vashti refused to come. Then the king became furious and burned with anger.

—Esther 1:12

What if our actions, in alignment with our convictions, set the stage for another to thrive? What if a woman we've never met and never will meet is able to pursue redemption and wholeness because we stuck to our principles? Because we refused to budge? Because our "no" meant "no"?

In the book of Esther, Queen Vashti's refusal to be ogled by drunken men set in motion a rescue plan even before Esther had entered the scene. Queen Vashti came first. She was more than a convenient reason as to why there was a vacancy in the palace—later to be filled by

Esther. She was a woman the earth had been waiting for, eons ahead of her time.

Long before she stood up to her husband-king at a dinner party, another banquet, years before, proved just as tragic for her. According to a Midrashic account, young Vashti was orphaned after her father, Belshazzar, ruler of Babylon, was crushed by a candelabrum while hosting a royal dinner. World leaders Cyrus the Persian and Darius the Mede just so happened to be among the guests of honor. Amid the panic, young Vashti sought out her father only to find Darius sitting in her dad's customary chair. Darius claimed her as his own and betrothed her to his son, Ahasuerus (the Hebrew name for Xerxes).[1] In a single night, at a dinner party among selfish men, her world was turned upside down. To her dismay, history would repeat itself.

Years later, as the wife of King Xerxes, Queen Vashti was forbidden by law from appearing publicly. She was out of sight, limited to an existence within approved chambers of the palace—until one night when her drunken husband dictated otherwise. After a week of indulgent feasting with an open bar, the inebriated king decided to put his power on display by parading his beautiful queen before a host of other intoxicated men. The Talmud suggests that the crowd insisted on Queen Vashti appearing before them nude.[2] Never mind that the law forbade them from seeing her even fully clothed. Despite King Xerxes sending not one, not two, but seven eunuchs to fetch his bride, it was a hard pass for Queen Vashti. She wouldn't be the final act of his seven-day drunken feast. His political prowess and reign over 127 provinces stretching from

India to Ethiopia seemingly weren't enough to make him feel validated, but apparently openly objectifying a woman was.

Queen Vashti's refusal was seen as public defiance of her husband and political resistance to a head of state. Like his next wife, Esther, she was orphaned and trapped in a patriarchal system that dictated where she could go and what she could wear. Yet she held tightly to her dignity. Rather than reconsider his ridiculous command, the likely still inebriated King Xerxes consulted his royal aides and billed Queen Vashti's action as treason. They feared Vashti's refusal might lead to devastating consequences for the kingdom at large: one in which women might wish to have autonomy over their own bodies. Queen Vashti upset gender norms in a society committed to the subjugation of women; for that, it appeared that the only reasonable option was banishment.

Esther 1:15–20 details Queen Vashti's fall from grace:

> "What must be done to Queen Vashti?" the king demanded. "What penalty does the law provide for a queen who refuses to obey the king's orders, properly sent through his eunuchs?"
>
> Memucan answered the king and his nobles, "Queen Vashti has wronged not only the king but also every noble and citizen throughout your empire. Women everywhere will begin to despise their husbands when they learn that Queen Vashti has refused to appear before the king. Before this day is out, the wives of all the king's nobles throughout Persia and Media will hear what the queen did and will start treating their husbands the same way. There will be no end to their contempt and anger.

"So if it please the king, we suggest that you issue a written decree, a law of the Persians and Medes that cannot be revoked. It should order that Queen Vashti be forever banished from the presence of King Xerxes, and that the king should choose another queen more worthy than she. When this decree is published throughout the king's vast empire, husbands everywhere, whatever their rank, will receive proper respect from their wives!" (NLT)

Vashti's courageous refusal was painted as a threat to national stability, as her apparent disrespect might entice other women to despise their husbands. Author Timothy Beal explains, "Like a pebble dropped in a puddle, the queen's offense is first against the king, but moves out 'against all the chiefs,' reverberating through every concentric ring of power, ultimately threatening the entire sexual-political order."[3] It's wild to think that one woman might potentially unravel the entire social order of the Persian Empire.

Without Vashti's decision and subsequent banishment, there would be no Queen Esther, no request before her erratic husband to spare her people. Both women had principles that could have cost them their lives. Vashti refused to appear before the king, and Esther dared appear without being summoned. Judaic scholar Yvonne Sherwood notes, "If we place Vashti and Esther side by side, we see that this book provides us with two clear types of female resistance in the face of male absolute power. The first type, performed by Vashti, is direct confrontation, while the second type, performed by Esther, is more familiar from biblical literature and is characterized by *arum*, pragmatism. In sum, while

Vashti refuses to display her physical beauty, Esther deliberately cultivates her physical beauty as a means to her end: gaining liberation for her people."[4] Both women embodied honor and self-respect, and while they're never in the same scene, their stories are forever intertwined. Maybe both women were created for such a time as that, following in the lineage of brave women who challenged power-hungry men and broken systems, who cracked glass ceilings and made headway for all to flourish. Their interwoven stories remind us that our courage could pave the way for another to play her part, faithfully living by her convictions and commitments.

In our moment in history, our acts of courage and our defiance against systems not built for us are interconnected to renew, restore, resurrect, and refresh many more people than we can know.

PRAYER

God of Queen Vashti,
give me the courage to stand my
ground against injustice.
God of Queen Esther,
allow me to see how others have made
a way for my story to unfold.

• • •

DECLARATION

Living by my convictions makes space
for the renewal of others,
as I commit to goodness for all.

QUESTIONS TO PONDER

- What matriarchs in your lineage modeled a commitment to their convictions?
- What has that meant to you?

21

The Stories
We Tell Ourselves

But watch yourselves! Otherwise, your heart might be
led astray so you stray away, serving other gods and
worshipping them.

—Deuteronomy 11:16 (CEB)

The stories we tell ourselves hold tremendous weight.
They determine our behavior, trigger emotional and
physical responses, and, more often than not, we so-
lidify them as fact in our minds. Yet some of those
stories could be lies masquerading as truth, deceiving
us and destroying others. As a rule, if the stories we tell
ourselves end with a justification for trampling over the
rights of another person, we've lost our way.

In Genesis 16, Sarai insists on using Hagar's body as
a means to an end, convincing herself she must write
Abram's legacy story rather than trust in the timing
of the Divine.

If she is to be the progenitor of all Israel sans heir, it seems only right to produce a baby by whatever means possible—even if that means forcing an Egyptian slave girl to lay with her husband. Surrogacy was a common practice of Mesopotamian influence and an apparent fit for Sarai. Entering the winter of her life, she borrows someone else's womb to accomplish God's grand plan, as the Lord had told Abram his heir would be *his* flesh and blood. Her husband had been promised offspring as numerous as the stars, despite her child-bearing years being long behind her. When the enslaved girl becomes pregnant with Abram's baby, she grows to despise Sarai, and Sarai retaliates with contempt.

In a situation of her own making, Sarai believed the story she told herself—that she must fulfill what only God could accomplish.

We may not bow before the gods of ancient times, but the siren of security sings to us, calling us to pursue what we believe to be *the way* even if it means stepping over others to do it. Perhaps we can't help but tell ourselves a story in which we star as the hero, a hero who at all costs pursues their mission no matter the means to that end. Viola Davis, in her memoir, *Finding Me*, remarks, "Show me the hero. Show me the tragedy. Heroes always cause their own downfalls." According to Deuteronomy 11:16, without a commitment to humility we're destined to lose our way and stray from God's path.

Women throughout history have been swayed by nationalism, elitism, classism, and racism—just as we are in this modern day. Persuasive arguments that scratch away at the beliefs embodied by our ancestors seduce us to worship at the altar of power and control. The stories we tell ourselves that motivate our actions are influenced by geography, faith tradition, political affiliation, class, race, ethnicity, gender, and what we think we and our community deserve. Even if it means using another, like an enslaved Egyptian.

The stories that occupy our minds define our existence and affect others. One patron saint of being honest, Anne Lamott, shares, "The *stories we tell ourselves* and write can warp us or raise us, save or destroy us, illuminate or dissemble."[3] These stories reveal our innermost workings and set the trajectory for our future. We must be accountable for how these stories shape our world. As Proverbs says, "As he thinketh in his heart, so is he" (23:7 KJV).

As a spiritual discipline, we can heed the warning in Deuteronomy to watch ourselves, question our motives, and turn from the gods that call us away from the Divine. We are part of a collective story, the one that is written until our last breath. If the story strays from the cowriter's direction, we miss the majesty of humility, of God's hand in and through us for purposes beyond our comprehension—purposes unbound by exceptionalism and hierarchy. The women we've been waiting for tell themselves stories born not out of fear, security, or control but out of love.

PRAYER

God of Those Who Stray,
give me eyes to see the error of my ways.
God of Redemption,
grant me grace when I get it wrong.

DECLARATION

I will seek to partner with others
rather than use them.
I will seek to include others rather
than segregate them.
I will seek to befriend others rather than vilify them.

• • •

QUESTIONS TO PONDER

- Have you found yourself making excuses for decisions that could potentially belittle another?

- What stories have you observed about other people groups that robbed them of their inherent dignity? What would it take to dismantle these ideas in the stories you tell yourself?

22

Waiting

When they arrived, they went upstairs to the room where they were staying. Those present were Peter, John, James and Andrew; Philip and Thomas, Bartholomew and Matthew; James son of Alphaeus and Simon the Zealot, and Judas son of James. They all joined together constantly in prayer, along with the women and Mary the mother of Jesus, and with his brothers.

—Acts 1:13–14

Who we become in times of waiting might determine more of our story than we anticipate. And as much as we'd like to take a shortcut to get where we want to go, waiting offers us space to develop a discipline of deep trust in the Divine.

The psalmist spoke to *how* we should wait as we follow God: "Wait patiently for the LORD. Be brave and courageous. Yes, wait patiently for the LORD" (Ps. 27:14

NLT). Later, the psalmist adds that we wait in hope (33:20). We aren't to wait with frantic anticipation but patiently and with hope—a tall order in our present day of lightning-fast delivery and instant coffee. Yet the gifts of waiting are not to be underrated. The prophet Isaiah calls those who wait on the Lord for help blessed (Isa. 30:18) and recipients of strength (40:31).

Waiting well is an opportunity to trust that the Divine is at work and that the cosmic forces that fashioned heaven and earth will intercede on our behalf, guiding the story for the better. But as we all well know, waiting on the Lord can take a dark turn if we let doubt trample our hope, if we let our unbelief sully and sour our reliance on the Faithful One. At times we might feel waiting is an exercise in futility and, like Sarai, try to write the ending to the story ourselves because we find God slow to act. But if her story teaches us anything, it's that waiting is par for the course.

Hannah waited for her womb to swell with a baby after years of infertility.

Ruth waited for her kinsman-redeemer to care for her and her mother-in-law.

Mary, the mother of Jesus, waited in the upper room among the early believers, anticipating the gift her son promised.

In Acts 1:13–14, a record of who was in the room on Pentecost includes Mary and other women. I can only imagine what this full-circle moment meant to her. She carried and raised the Divine enfleshed, witnessed his gruesome death, celebrated his resurrection, and then on that glorious day she received the Spirit for herself. She'd waited since her adolescent years for all that God had promised her. She couldn't rush it, although she was more than ready for the world to witness her son's glory at the wedding in Cana. All things considered, much of her adult life was one of waiting for the presence of God manifested in her son to usher in a new kingdom. No small wait!

As we learn from Hannah, Ruth, and Mary, *how* we wait is as important as *what* we wait for.

Hannah wept in the temple, honest and desperate tears pouring down her cheeks as she waited for God to answer her prayers for a baby.

Ruth gleaned from the fields and made herself available, waiting for Boaz to do right by her family.

Mary assisted her beloved son in his ministry and stood by his side in his final hours, waiting for his kingdom to come.

Waiting leaves us at the mercy of God's divine schedule, refusing to move or act before we sense God's nudge. Elisabeth Elliot explains, "Waiting on God requires the willingness to bear uncertainty, to carry within oneself the unanswered question, lifting the heart to God about it whenever it intrudes upon one's thoughts. It's easy to talk oneself into a decision that has no permanence—easier sometimes than to wait patiently."[1] It's humbling to admit we're not in control of our own destiny and to yield the pen to the One greater than ourselves who might write the story slower than we'd prefer. But let's remember the blessings reserved for those that Isaiah spoke of. We may feel passed over, rejected, or ignored, but our deep trust develops the maturity that reminds us that God is faithful and that our waiting isn't a sign of indifference or laziness. It's a practice that recognizes our limits and trusts that God is writing the story of our lives.

PRAYER

God of Hannah,
you know the deepest desires of my heart
and meet me in my time of sorrow.
God of Ruth,
I will wait on you as you provide for my every need.
God of Mary,
I will allow my seasons of waiting to
forge me into a formidable woman.

• • •

DECLARATION

I trust that you see me in my seasons of waiting.

• • •

QUESTIONS TO PONDER

- How has waiting on the Lord challenged and formed you?
- On what issues do you recognize you need to wait on God rather than intervene?

23

Who Is Pure?

ANGIE KAY HONG

We always carry around in our body the death of Jesus, so that the life of Jesus may also be revealed in our body. For we who are alive are always being given over to death for Jesus' sake, so that his life may also be revealed in our mortal body. So then, death is at work in us, but life is at work in you.

—2 Corinthians 4:10–12

They were called "comfort women," as if they served hot cocoa and handed out warm blankets to tired and weary soldiers after a long day of battle. It was even said that they willingly signed up to live in comfort stations, as if to sell goods in merchant stalls. As if.

During World War II, an estimated two hundred thousand women and girls from Korea, China, and other Asian countries were kidnapped by the Japanese military and forced into sexual slavery. Day after day, from 1932 through 1945, these comfort women were beaten, tortured, and raped on a regular basis by Japanese soldiers. Imprisoned in comfort stations where they were separated by curtains or thin walls, they were treated as both objects to derive pleasure from and objects to display hatred toward the weak and colonized. Many comfort women died from disease, malnutrition, or violent wounds. Some even took their own lives to escape their unbearable conditions. Those who managed to survive the war returned to their hometowns only to find decimated cities and scattered relatives.

Regardless of whether they had family or not, the remaining comfort women in Korea were rejected and shunned, judged and shamed for the rest of their lives. Their pasts were now reminders of weakness. Many lived in abject poverty, isolated from the rest of society and forced to hide their histories to avoid being judged. One by one, each comfort woman died in silence, never speaking of the horror-filled events that haunted them for the rest of their lives.

Second Corinthians reminds us that Jesus had a physical body. He was God in human form, with skin, bones, hair, teeth, muscles, fatty tissue, facial hair, armpits, and eyelashes. The tips of his fingers rubbed the grooves in wood, intuiting the direction of the grain and sanding it down until it was level and smooth. His skin wrinkled and puffed up as he humbly washed each of the twelve disciples' calloused feet. His own feet blistered when he broke in new sandals. His heart thumped wildly during the last meal with his closest friends as he requested that they remember him.

And then, Jesus's body felt the shame and humiliation heaped on him by the crowds as he dragged his own heavy cross through the streets. His ears heard the judgment and insults flung at him. His hands and feet felt each painful nail as it was hammered through his flesh, and he tasted the sting of vinegar against his lips. His body felt the gruesome cruelty of a state-sanctioned death. With his last breath, his body went limp, slouching but pinned upright against the rough wood.

After the resurrection, Jesus's body was not smooth, glowing, or unblemished. He reappeared still bearing the scars of death and marks of humiliation. He held them up for Thomas and everyone to see. The marks were a part of him now; he spoke with them and through them for forty days before finally going home to heaven.

Christians have a tough time reckoning with their bodies. What do we do with them? What do we think of them? What does it mean to treat our bodies like temples? What do we wear? How do we take care of them? Does it matter what we look like, what gender we are, what race or ethnicity we are? And who is to blame if bad things happen to them? Or does none of that matter because we transcend our earthly bodies and focus on our identities in Christ?

We tend to think of purity as a melting away of our impurities. We are supposed to enter the refiner's fire, reemerging sanctified and spotless. But as Christ's resurrected body reminds us, we still carry the scars. Our scars are enmeshed with his as we move about the world.

We could allow our scars to cause us to feel shame and unworthiness. We could pretend the scars aren't there. Or we can remind ourselves that just as Jesus's body evidenced both death and life, so too can ours.

Hak-Sun Kim carried the horrible atrocities of being a comfort woman in her body. She bore her scars and wounds. She saw many die before her and after her in despair and silence. But something in her refused to accept a fate of silent shame. Something inside her refused to accept that her scars and wounds meant she had no place or voice in this world.

In 1991, more than forty years after her horrible experiences during the war, Hak-Sun gave the first ever public testimony about being a comfort woman. It was broadcast all over the world. She spared no details of the horrific things that happened to her. Later that year, Hak-Sun decided to take on the entire Japanese government and filed a lawsuit demanding reparations and apologies to the survivors.

Hak-Sun spoke courageously through her scars. Slowly, other survivors came forward and told their own stories of being comfort women. Women from China, Korea, and the Philippines emerged to tell the world about their own horrific experiences. All in all, around two hundred witnesses and survivors came forward and told their stories. Hak-Sun protested in the streets with the other women, demanding an apology and recognition of the injustice done to these women in history books. She published her story. Monuments were built all over the world in honor and in remembrance of her and the other survivors.

Hak-Sun Kim's decision to speak through her wounds and not deny them, hide them, or shrink away in silence and shame is evidence of a body carrying both death and life together, refusing to be separated from the scars inflicted through violence and hatred.

Jesus speaks to us today through the scars and wounds he bears. As Jesus followers, we have the privilege of doing the same. Some may even say it's a calling, but to others it is a way of being. We are made pure by the evidence of our scars and wounds. Let us speak and act through them.

PRAYER

Dear Divine and Scarred One,
thank you for speaking through your wounds.
I praise you for seeing my wounds.
Help me to speak through them.
Amen.

DECLARATION

I won't despise my wounds
or the wounds of others.
I'm wholly pure in the life and death of Christ.

QUESTIONS TO PONDER

- As you ponder on your body as a gift given by God, how do you relate to it? Treat it? Think about it?
- What would it mean for you to speak through your own wounds and scars boldly?
- How can you help others in how they treat and relate to their own bodies as gifts from God?

24

Despair and the Divine

You are the God who sees me.

—Genesis 16:13 (NLT)

Undoubtedly, in our moments of despair, many of us grapple with who the God of the Universe is.

Does God care?

Does God see us?

Does God know that our despair is more than we can bear?

The answer is yes, yes, and yes.

We certainly aren't the first to wrestle with these questions, and those who've gone before us offer insight that addresses the heart of the matter.

Hagar, an enslaved Egyptian woman, was forced to lay with Abram and then was despised for her growing belly. When Sarai's disdain reached a fever pitch, Hagar fled from her abusive mistress. She would take her chances with starvation, homelessness, and wandering through the desert—any path other than suffering under Sarai's authority. After all, it was her mistress's idea for Hagar to serve as a surrogate after years of infertility, yet Sarai wasn't satisfied when what she wanted to happen . . . happened.

Although Sarai's meddling in the plans of God backfired on her, the Giver of Life was in the shadows, prepared to meet Hagar in her despair. On the roadside by a spring of water, heaven collided with earth for the love of a woman.

> The angel said to her, "Hagar, Sarai's servant, where have you come from, and where are you going?"
>
> "I'm running away from my mistress, Sarai," she replied.
>
> The angel of the LORD said to her, "Return to your mistress, and submit to her authority." Then he added, "I will give you more descendants than you can count."
>
> And the angel also said, "You are now pregnant and will give birth to a son. You are to name him Ishmael (which means 'God hears'), for the LORD has heard your cry of distress. This son of yours will be a wild man, as untamed as a wild donkey! He will raise his fist against everyone, and everyone will be against him. Yes, he will live in open hostility against all his relatives."
>
> Thereafter, Hagar used another name to refer to the LORD, who had spoken to her. She said, "You are the God who sees me." She also said, "Have I truly seen the One who sees me?" (Gen. 16:8–13 NLT)

Although Abram and Sarai never call her by name in the Genesis 16 account, Hagar, with leading lady energy, boldly proclaimed that the Divine saw her, and she went back to her less-than-ideal situation knowing that God was looking out for her. In her moment of despair, she discovered she was far from alone, and the unfolding plan was much greater than she could have imagined. In a time when honor was tied to lineage, an enslaved woman was promised numerous descendants, just as Abram was.

Notably, the angel of the Lord appeared to many leaders in Israel's history; yet, before counseling them, the angel appeared to an enslaved Egyptian woman pregnant with her master's baby who had been mistreated by her mistress. She held lesser status in the eyes of her masters but was equally beloved by the Divine, and Hagar's despair was the seedbed for her destiny. Mary Elizabeth Baxter notes, "Hagar came into the liberty which belonged to those who recognize the presence of God."[1] Still, Hagar knew as well as any of us do that the presence of the Divine does not assume a despair-free existence. She was subject to a system of oppression, ostracized by her household, looked upon as a foreigner, and was the only one looking after the interests of her son. Later, in Genesis 21, Hagar was forced out of her home and sent into the wilderness, and once again, Hagar witnessed the angel of the Lord as she despaired.

> So Abraham got up early the next morning, prepared food and a container of water, and strapped them on Hagar's shoulders. Then he sent her away with their son, and she wandered aimlessly in the wilderness of Beersheba.
>
> When the water was gone, she put the boy in the shade of a bush. Then she went and sat down by her-

self about a hundred yards away. "I don't want to watch the boy die," she said, as she burst into tears.

But God heard the boy crying, and the angel of God called to Hagar from heaven, "Hagar, what's wrong? Do not be afraid! God has heard the boy crying as he lies there. Go to him and comfort him, for I will make a great nation from his descendants."

Then God opened Hagar's eyes, and she saw a well full of water. She quickly filled her water container and gave the boy a drink.

And God was with the boy as he grew up in the wilderness. He became a skillful archer, and he settled in the wilderness of Paran. His mother arranged for him to marry a woman from the land of Egypt. (Gen. 21:14–21 NLT)

As it did for Hagar, the divinity discovered in our despair may help us recognize that our individual experiences, however sordid or tragic, are never beyond redemption. In their book *Truth's Table*, Ekemini Uwan, Christina Edmondson, and Michelle Higgins note, "God's deep and abiding, steadfast love, promised a justice that Hagar would never have found in the tents of Abraham. She was brought out to build a nation free from enslavement, and free from the threat of her body being misused. Covenant justice means that the Lord sees us. All of us."[2] Despair may be weaved through our stories, but the greater narrative is one of wholeness and goodness, repair and restoration.

At the same time, within our despair, we discover who the Divine is and is not. We discover the difference between what God intends to do and what we *think* God should do. Priest and theologian Ronald Rolheiser explains: "When we break down, it's not the real God we despair of, but only God as we imagined him. What we feel in emptiness is not the death of God but rather the space within which God can be born. What loneliness and despair deprive us of is not God, but our illusions about God. The finite, not the infinite, is what's taken from us."[3] Holding the paradox of Divine Presence and despair hardly feels like an act of self-care, but it most certainly is. Grasping the idea that seemingly opposed truths are simultaneously true is embodied wisdom. Hagar's story models this tension—a tension to be managed, not solved. It makes evident that despair and the Divine Presence coexist, and as Rolheiser notes, the former does not rob us of the latter. Our distress does not assume God's absence, only that the Divine Presence may not act or do as we'd hoped. The Divine is unpredictable, unbridled, and may have a better ending to our despair than we could imagine.

PRAYER

God of Mother Hagar,
help me to find your divine
presence within my despair.
God of Desert Places,
you are the one who sees me.

• • •

DECLARATION

I am loved by the God who sees me
and is ever present in my distress.

QUESTIONS TO PONDER

- Who have you discovered God *not* to be in your despair?
- How have you witnessed the presence of God within your despairing times?

PART 4

FORMATION
OF THE
SOUL

I have to constantly re-identify myself to myself, reactivate my own standards, my own convictions about what I'm doing and why.

—Nina Simone

25

Collateral Damage

By so much, Jesus has become the collateral of a better covenant.

—Hebrews 7:22 (WEB)

A woman's value is nonnegotiable. Yet too often the world acts as though it is. Women are commonly treated as bargaining chips, pawns, or means to an end. Worse, many of us have internalized this treatment as normal.

In 2014, #bringbackourgirls was trending on social media worldwide in response to Nigerian women and girls being abducted by the rebel group Boko Haram. Used as sex slaves, human shields, and suicide bombers, they were considered expendable in what the jihadist group deemed a "holy war." In Nigeria's Borno State, three hundred girls were kidnapped from a single school and used as a bargaining chip in political negotiations. Afterward, for fear of abduction, girls dropped out of school, furthering illiteracy rates in an already androcentric society that limits women's civic and social engagement.[1] Women and girls suffered at Boko Haram's hands both directly and indirectly.

Unsurprisingly, women have been treated as wartime collateral damage since ancient times. In the Scriptures, Judges 11 offers the grim story of Jephthah, a Gileadite commander against the Ammonites, who swore to Yahweh that if he was awarded victory in battle, he'd offer as a burnt offering whoever (or whatever) came out of his house upon his return.[2] After he defeats his foes, he returns home the conquering victor, but his joy quickly melts into sorrow when his daughter and only child runs out to greet him with dancing and timbrels. Her life would be his celebratory sacrifice.

At the hands of Boko Haram or Jephthah, or a thousand battles in between, in the theater of war women and girls are acceptable collateral damage. Honor killings, child marriages, sexual assault, acid attacks, and countless other acts against women transpire in wartime and in peacetime. Because they are considered more of a liability than an asset, their suffering has been inevitable, and power players know this to be true. In 2011, an anonymous senior White House official commented on Afghan women's treatment during the Afghanistan War: "Gender issues are going to have to take a back seat to other priorities. There's no way we can be successful if we maintain every special interest and pet project. All those pet rocks in our rucksack were taking us down." In response, Kathleen Parker posed the question in the *Washington Post*, "What if saving women from cultures that treat them as chattel was in our strategic and not just moral interest? What if helping women become equal members of society was the most reliable route to our own security?" She added, "The insanity that sends jihadists to rain hell on civilized nations is the same that stones women to death for failing to comply with primitive norms of behavior."[3] As Parker implies, women's formation is part of the answer we've been waiting for.

In a world that far too easily offers up women as collateral damage, Jesus modeled a different way. In his upside-down kingdom, women are worthy of protection *and* a peaceable future we can all inhabit by design. Our physical, psychological, sexual, and social safety is precious in his sight, as evidenced by John 8. As Jesus taught a crowd in the temple, the Pharisees famously threw an alleged adulterous woman at his feet to see how he'd respond. Would he dismiss her without paying any mind to the Pharisees? Would he act in defiance of the laws of the day? Would he be inconsistent with his teachings? Would he fall for the trap set by selfish men who found his compassion offensive? Jesus's reaction would be fodder for their case against him. This woman's life was simply a means to an end, but Jesus had other plans for her.

> Jesus stooped down and wrote in the dust with his finger. They kept demanding an answer, so he stood up again and said, "All right, but let the one who has never sinned throw the first stone!" Then he stooped down again and wrote in the dust.
>
> When the accusers heard this, they slipped away one by one, beginning with the oldest, until only Jesus was left in the middle of the crowd with the woman.

Then Jesus stood up again and said to the woman, "Where are your accusers? Didn't even one of them condemn you?"

"No, Lord," she said.

And Jesus said, "Neither do I. Go and sin no more." (John 8:6–11 NLT)

When asked to assess their actions, the crowd left one by one. No one would be stoned to death. Nor would the holy man be arrested. The value of this woman— her bones and blood, memories and stories, family and future—was nonnegotiable in the eyes of Christ. The Pharisees made the moment about using her as a way to entrap Jesus, but Jesus made it all about *her* protection. Her safety and reputation held precedence. She wasn't a special interest or pet project sidelining his plan to usher in freedom for the captives; she was central to it. He would be the collateral damage in the story of our restoration, not her nor any other woman. To go and sin no more was a formative invitation to live outside the label with which society had branded her. She could live differently. Jesus's later exchanges with women in his company undergird this stance that women are valuable, central to the plan of his kingdom come, and never expendable. Their formation is foundational to communal renewal.

In a Western context, we're likely not fearful of stoning or abduction, but without agency, we may fall on the proverbial sword to ensure the continuation of broken systems because they are what we are accustomed to, or we might make ourselves small to be accepted. We offer ourselves as collateral damage without fully realizing it. If we've been conditioned to believe that we, as women, are the problem, through poor Scripture instruction or cultural scripts, it's nearly impossible to see ourselves as part of the solution. Our formation is forever stunted. Nevertheless, our spiritual and emotional growth is integral to healing abusive systems, communities, and nations. As we find our feet, steady our souls, and renew our minds, we see ourselves not as collateral damage but as crucial to the kingdom come.

We can push for an existence in which all of us see ourselves as reliable visionaries of the future, not as bodies to be exploited or as voices to be stifled. In our day, as we witness countless women sidelined, silenced, or sexually abused as faith leaders fight over who is worthy of power, or as politicians use women as pawns to gain ground, may we lean into the way of Jesus, protecting and empowering our mothers, sisters, friends, and daughters to live as coheirs, never collateral damage.

PRAYER

God of Nigeria's Daughters,
I honor the body and breath of
my sisters on the earth.
God of Jephthah's Daughter,
let me live out my days in love and care.

• • •

DECLARATION

My worth is nonnegotiable.
My life is a contribution toward communal renewal.

QUESTIONS TO PONDER

- How have you witnessed women set aside as collateral damage? In your community? Church? Workplace?

- In your spiritual, social, or professional context, how can you ensure women and girls are positioned as assets rather than liabilities?

26

We Remember You

ARIANA ALTIERY-RIVERA

The women said to Naomi, "Blessed be the Lord, who has not left you without a family redeemer today. May his name become well known in Israel. He will renew your life and sustain you in your old age. Indeed, your daughter-in-law, who loves you and is better to you than seven sons, has given birth to him."

—Ruth 4:14–15 (CSB)

To be a woman in this world is to endure pain and grief, to be constantly invited to bite into bitterness. We make our way forward understanding that life won't be easy, and it isn't supposed to be. While joy, abundance, and celebration are ours because of our loving God, this fallen world bites at our heels and hearts. Yet, thank God we are rarely alone. We stand alongside the women who've raised us, the women who grew up on our block, and the girlfriends who've been by our sides, and we are affectionately formed by their support.

In the book of Ruth, we learn of a family that falls apart after they leave home to escape famine. Naomi, a wife and mother, loses the three most important men in her life, one after the other. She becomes the de facto leader of her family, stranded with her two daughters-in-law, Ruth and Orpah. Widowed women in Naomi's time were without a place in society; they had no rights and no one to protect them. This was the case for Naomi, Ruth, and Orpah—all of them widowed and without a place to call home. Naomi urges her daughters-in-law to return to their families, hoping they will find new husbands. She believes that she has nothing to offer them now, that she isn't worth sticking around for. In her grief, she believes that without her husband and her sons she is a liability, as society had taught her. In reality, what Naomi still has is her God and God's blessings. God has not abandoned her.

Although she is from another land and culture, Ruth is devoted to Naomi. Ruth sees Naomi's value and boldly declares that she will not leave and that Naomi, even after all she has lost, is worth staying with and following.

> But Ruth replied: Don't plead with me to abandon you or to return and not follow you. For wherever you go, I will go, and wherever you live, I will live; your people will be my people, and your God will be my God. Where you die, I will die, and there I will be buried. May the LORD punish me, and do so severely,

if anything but death separates you and me. (Ruth 1:16–17 CSB, format modified)

Although this passage is often quoted in wedding ceremonies, it's not a declaration of romantic love. It's a statement of commitment made by one grieving woman to another grieving woman. Ruth sees Naomi as the beloved mother-in-law that she is, even though Naomi has almost completely lost sight of herself.

Upon Naomi's arrival back in her hometown, Scripture explains that the "local women" recognize her, celebrating her arrival, but Naomi tells everyone to call her by a new name, Mara, which means "bitter." She tells them she has been abandoned by God. Scripture doesn't tell us that the women argue with her. I imagine that they would've asked her what happened and why she believes she's been abandoned. I imagine them looking around, silently agreeing that they will revisit this confession later.

I've been on the receiving end of counsel from friends who've aided in my formation when I've lost sight of myself. Friends gathered over coffee with listening ears but with no intention of staying quiet when I tried to convince them that things were so bad that God no longer had anything to do with my story. I wonder how this scene played out for Naomi once she returned to the women who *knew* her, who would've raised her, and who witnessed God's blessing in her life before she left.

I'm so glad that Naomi went home to those "local women" during this time of her life. Who better to remind her of who she really is when she's lost sight of the woman she was. In bitter times, it's our "local women" who can point us back to our true identity, often better than anyone else. They remind us that we're forged by fire, formed by trying times.

Naomi's story continues like so many of ours do. She wrestles with the pain of disappointment, wondering about what life would've been like if things hadn't taken a turn for the worse. Yet beautiful things happen for her family; they are redeemed. Ruth remarries and a grandson is born to Naomi. As it did with Naomi, bitterness can blind us from looking ahead to the beauty of the next season after a particularly devastating one, but thank God that we have, and can become part of, the "local women" who name what's true when we've lost our way—women who call us by our names, remind us of God's hand over our lives, and name the blessings to come.

Like Naomi, we are not what we've lost, although we are undoubtedly formed by our losses. In bitter times, when we lose sight of the good trajectory of our story, we can listen to those who know us. We can admit there was always someone by our side, that the *Ruths* with us are more valuable than all the sons. We can allow our "local women" to speak plainly of our blessings and remind us of what's true.

PRAYER

God Who Knows Me,
remind me of your love and purpose for my life.
God of My Beautiful and Bitter Times,
send me to the women who need
to be reminded of your care.

DECLARATION

Grief and loss cannot rename my friends.
I will remember who they are and
remind them of their goodness.

. . .

QUESTIONS TO PONDER

- How can you respond with love and truth when your friend is losing sight of herself?
- Who are you allowing to speak honestly to you in your bitter times?

27

Magnificent Refuge

You who sit down in the High God's presence,
   spend the night in Shaddai's shadow,
Say this: "GOD, you're my refuge.
   I trust in you and I'm safe!"
                              —Psalm 91:1–2 (Message)

There is a safe and refreshing place available to all of us who call on the Lord. A space not found on a map with a physical address but a space within. Within this space we do not need to *do* anything; we only need to *be*. We are invited to come as we are. When we find this space and visit often, we're never the same. We emerge from it as our fullest selves. In the sixteenth century, a Carmelite nun discovered this secret place, and no one could stop her from visiting, not even naysayers within the church.

As a tenacious seven-year-old, young Teresa ran away with her brother Rodrigo in hopes of martyrdom, but they made it only as far as the town walls before their uncle escorted them home. Teresa's mother was devoted to God, and Teresa listened intently to every word her beloved mother instructed on matters of faith. When her mother died four years later, Teresa turned to Mother Mary as her source of encouragement.

After Teresa finished her education, her uncle urged her to join the Carmelite Convent of the Incarnation in Ávila, Spain. Not long after, she fell terribly ill and spent the better part of her remaining life battling convulsions, stomach pains, loss of consciousness, and dizziness.[1] As her physical and mental maladies developed, so did her love of contemplative prayer in the convent. At the time, church leaders didn't believe women were capable of communing with God in prayer on their own: they needed guidance. Sixteenth-century theologians were under the influence of Aristotle, who believed women were ruled by passion rather than reason and therefore were disqualified from the seriousness prayer required. Teresa claimed God gave her visions and understanding that baffled her contemporaries. Kieran Kavanaugh remarks on Teresa's predicament: "The theologians who directed Teresa could not understand how a woman, especially one as imperfect as Teresa presented herself to be, could receive such favors from God. These could only be an illusion from the devil. No wonder Teresa thought so little of herself. She didn't feel capable of much."[2] The Middle Ages' unique brand of sexism and ableism forged the Carmelite nun's spiritual formation into something admirable and downright durable. Prayer became her secret place, her magnificent refuge where she became her truest self, made whole by the love of God and undeterred by haters. She held the door open for her sisters to do the same.

When prayer books were banned during the Spanish Inquisition, Teresa wrote not one but two books for her Carmelite sisters on finding unity with the Divine. She was convinced they could find equality in the eyes of God if only they would enter into God's presence. Teresa explained to her fellow sisters in *The Interior Castle*:

> There is a secret place. A radiant sanctuary. As real as your own kitchen. More real than that. Constructed of the purest elements. Overflowing with the ten thousand beautiful things. Worlds within worlds. Forests, rivers. Velvet coverlets thrown over featherbeds, fountains bubbling beneath a canopy of stars. Bountiful forests, universal libraries. A wine cellar offering an intoxication so sweet you will never be sober again. A clarity so complete you will never again forget. This magnificent refuge is inside you. Enter. Shatter the darkness that shrouds the doorway. . . . Believe the incredible truth that the Beloved has chosen for his dwelling place the core of your own being because that is the single most beautiful place in all of creation.[3]

Teresa believed union with the Divine came by deep, uninterrupted awareness of God's love for us. There is nothing we need to *do*, we only need to *be* in the glorious presence. So taken was she that the love of God was theirs to savor, she found the spiritual laxity of her convent unacceptable and sought permission to reform the order so she could transform women's awareness of their relation to God. She was awarded approval from her superiors and spent much of her life starting convents and monasteries devoted to prayer. Some of her contemporaries considered her a fraud, while others, including King Philip II of Spain, admired her and ensured she continued her ministry after church leaders attempted to force her into retirement. She was not a pushover in her efforts to reform the Carmelite Order and ruffled many feathers as she practiced dissent against her male counterparts. Teresa of Ávila, as she came to be known, was a mother of the monastic tradition. She urged not just those in the order but all men and women to embrace the presence of God in contemplative prayer.

With an endless cycle of bad news, stress, and anxiety weighing heavy upon us, Teresa's invitation is as timely as ever. We can center within, silence our minds, and enter stillness, giving ourselves fully to the presence without rattling off requests. Thomas Merton explains that contemplative prayer is not so much about finding God as about resting in the God we've already found, who loves us, who is near to us, and who comes to us to draw us to Godself.[4] In the presence of the Divine, we come as we are. Without agenda or expectation, we abide. Like Teresa, we can affirm that the Divine's presence isn't limited to the religious elite but is available to all: the worn-out, the tired, and the weary. The broken-bodied and broken-hearted are welcomed into the interior place where our souls are nourished by the God of the Universe without instruction. As we enter the magnificent refuge, we develop a steadfast spirit to bring back with us into our daily lives.

Teresa of Ávila's final encouragement in *The Interior Castle* reads, "In sum, my Sisters, what I conclude with is we shouldn't build castles in the air—but during the little while this life lasts, and perhaps it will last a shorter time than each one thinks, let us offer the Lord interiorly and exteriorly the sacrifice we can."[5] Her benediction to her sisters is one we can receive and take to heart. One that soberly reminds us of how short life is and how the presence of the Divine shapes not only our souls but also our actions. Teresa was certainly a woman history waited for, and as we seek renewal in our lives, like her, let us do so by practicing contemplative prayer, resting in the magnificent refuge of Shaddai's shadow.

PRAYER

God of Teresa of Ávila,
grant me your tender presence.
God of the Carmelite Sisters,
let no one keep me from your dwelling place.

• • •

DECLARATION

I will fearlessly do what is best.
All things pass. God does not change.

• • •

QUESTIONS TO PONDER

- How would you describe your interior castle?
- What would it take to build time into your calendar to visit as often as possible?

28

Navigating Burnout

KAYLA CRAIG

Let us not become weary in doing good, for at the proper time we will reap a harvest if we do not give up.
—Galatians 6:9

To care about injustice is lonely. To keep caring about it is even lonelier.

Ida B. Wells knew this exhausting loneliness deep in her bones. She knew what it was to feel the fiery edges of burnout growing, working to engulf the passion she used for good. A Black woman known for being a courageous journalist and determined crusader against the profound evils of racism at the turn of the century, Ida fueled her heart for justice to work for the flourishing of all people, even when she was the only one willing to lead the cause. When she put pen to paper, she spoke truth to power, bringing deep oppression and injustice into the light.

Time after time, she had reason after reason to let herself succumb to the flames of burnout that often press in on women who commit to doing the deep, lonely work of holding people accountable, dismantling oppressive systems, and working tirelessly to get others to care—as well as join in doing something about it.

To understand what undergirded her strength in the face of burnout, and what we might learn in light of that, we look to her beginnings and the woman who raised her.

When Ida was born in Mississippi in 1862, her parents were enslaved. Under the cruelties of slavery, her mother's faith led her to deeply held convictions about the "essential dignity" of all people.[1] Though both her parents died while Ida was still a teenager, leaving her with seven younger siblings to care for (the youngest just nine months old), the faith and fire her mother sparked in her continued to burn strong.

As Ida's youngest daughter wrote of her mother, she "began openly carrying her torch against lynching."[2] She stepped into her life's work not just to end the violent murders of Black men, women, and children but also to illuminate the many systemic inequities that plagued the country.

Though it's easy to lionize historical leaders like Ida, in doing so we ignore the fullness of their humanity. When we turn our eyes away from the anger and sorrow that weighed on them as they carried the banner of justice, we believe that we too must never cry out, grieve, step back, or rest.

Ida was mocked and maligned in newspapers. She was called militant, aggressive, and worse.[3] At just twenty-five years of age, she sued a railroad for not allowing her access to a first-class coach and won, only to have a judge overturn the case. She wrote this in her journal:

> I have firmly believed all along that the law was on our side and would, when we appealed to it, give us justice. I feel shorn of that belief and utterly discouraged, and just now, if it were possible, would gather my race in my arms and fly away with them. O God, is there no redress, no peace, no justice in this land for us? Thou hast always fought the battles of the weak and oppressed. Come to my aid at this moment and teach me what to do, for I am sorely, bitterly disappointed. Show us the way, even as Thou led the children of Israel out of bondage into the promised land.[4]

Ida took time to lament: to name her pain, to grieve deep inequities, and to call on the One she believed to be entirely just and dependable. Naming our pain and inviting God into the fullness of our humanity is a step toward preventing burnout, remembering with a stubborn hope that God does not forsake us in our suffering.

Isaiah wrote this to the people of Israel: "When you walk through the fire, you will not be burned; the flames will not set you ablaze" (Isa. 43:2). Naming pain allows us to begin to move through it. Rhythms of rest, community, and joy are balms against burnout.

As for Ida, she grieved, prayed, and did not relent. She moved forward, devoting her life to building the foundations of civil rights in the United States—even when she was the only one rolling up her sleeves to do so. Though she burned with passion to do the work, she (like generations of women after her) also worked to prioritize other parts of her life. For her, this meant stepping away for a season while she was in the thick of mothering four children. When she entered back into her advocacy and writing, she cared for her spiritual health (and the health of others in her community) by spending ten years teaching a weekly Bible study for more than a hundred young adult men.

Balance is a myth; like all of us, Ida spent her life figuring out healthy rhythms within her work, family, spiritual, and physical life. Once, her body was pushed to heal too fast after surgery, and physical and emotional recovery took more than a year. In her autobiography, she reflects on this season, writing, "During that year I did more serious thinking from a personal point of view than ever before in my life. All at once the realization came to me that I had nothing to show for all those years of toil and labor."[5]

From the outside, her profound leadership was tireless. Her impact was limitless. But behind the scenes, she was weary, wondering if anything she did mattered.

In 1897, Norman B. Wood said that when he looked at Ida and watched her plead the case for justice and fair treatment, he saw God raising up a modern Deborah, the fierce Old Testament judge who courageously led the people of Israel, advocating for them with strength and wisdom (Judg. 4). He wrote that perhaps God had protected Ida so that "she might light a flame of righteous indignation in England and America which, by God's grace, will never be extinguished."[6]

Caring about inequities and working for change can be lonely. At every turn, others will try to extinguish your light. But with God's help, the fields of flourishing you've planted will grow and multiply. You might not see the fruit in your lifetime, but your work matters, and so do *you*.

May God grant you rhythms of body and soul rest, protecting you from burnout so that you may continue to do the work God has set out for you.

PRAYER

God of Ida,
may your flame never be extinguished in me.
O God of Justice and Truth,
protect my mind, body, and soul from burning out.

• • •

DECLARATION

I love because God first loved me.
In light of this divine love, I will
care for the vulnerable.
I will co-labor with Christ for a
world where peace prevails.
I will fuel my fire to work for the
flourishing of all, including myself.

QUESTIONS TO PONDER

- What warning signs does your body give when you're on the verge of burnout?
- What sustainable rhythms of self-care can you add to your days?
- Why are boundaries important in preventing burnout?

29

Righteous Defiance

In fact, if you know the right thing to do and don't do it, that, for you, is evil.

—James 4:17 (Message)

What happens when the right thing to do is also the hardest? Or what if we have no guarantee that our right choices will be honored? What if the righteous next step on one's journey will put us in someone else's crosshairs?

What if, in some circumstances, "unladylike" defiance is actually holy?

Two fibbing midwives, Shiphrah and Puah, model righteous defiance when they defy Pharaoh's orders to commit Hebrew genocide by slaying the baby boys they deliver (Exod. 1:8–22). They had no plans to end life when they'd been trained to welcome it, and they revered the God of the Universe more than the king of

Egypt. Likely telling very few people, if anyone, about their plan to spare baby boys, they resumed the very same work as they had done before. When asked by Pharaoh why they were unsuccessful in committing infanticide, they cited the Hebrew women's quick births. A clever fib to mask treason.

Notably, the midwives had zero indication that their efforts would be rewarded. In fact, their defiance could have ended very poorly for them, but it didn't. Exodus 1:20–21 tells us, "God was good to the midwives, and the Israelites continued to multiply, growing more and more powerful. And because the midwives feared God, he gave them families of their own" (NLT). While the midwives were gifted families, verse 22 says that others were torn apart. Pharaoh ordered that every baby boy be thrown in the Nile River. The midwives likely knew Pharaoh would find a way to commit his heinous crimes and that their efforts would only delay him, but they'd have no part—passive or active—in his horrific plans no matter what happened to them. David Daube observes that this account is "the oldest record in world literature of the spurning of a governmental decree,"[1] notably without violent acts, but with the accessory of a birthing stool. Their convictions drove their quiet protest against the systemic injustice of their time. Hebrew women from eons ago understood defiance is not at odds with goodness for communal renewal; they're intertwined. Formation can take place by way of defiance.

In September 2022, nationwide protests broke out in Iran after twenty-two-year-old Mahsa Amini died in police custody. Authorities had arrested Mahsa for allegedly violating Islamic dress codes, claiming her hijab was too loose as some of her hair was exposed. Eyewitnesses who were detained with her reported that she was severely beaten, and she fell into a coma, dying soon after. Once word of her arrest and mistreatment went public, protestors burned their hijabs in the streets while authorities attempted to disperse them with tear gas, water cannons, and metal pellets. Undaunted, young protestors voiced dissent and were arrested themselves.[2] From the north to the south, their chant of resistance against regime leader Ali Khamenei could be heard. Khamenei insisted on controlling women's bodies by force, and Gen Z Iranian women and girls refused to be dominated without defiance.

Iran's *Gasht-e-Ershad* (guidance patrol), commonly known as the morality police, roam the streets arresting women and girls who wear ripped jeans, fitted clothes, shorts, sleeves rolled up, or, as in Mahsa's case, wear their hijab too loosely. In protest of the *Gasht-e-Ershad*, women have donned red lipstick, worn all white on Wednesdays sans hijab, and developed an app that tracks police checkpoints based on shared user data.[3]

Their protest has had little to do with religion and everything to do with human rights, because it wasn't always like this. Mandated head coverings in Iran took effect in 1979 after the Islamic Revolution overthrew the modern monarchy. Before the revolution, women wore hijabs *in protest* of the monarchy's ideals. In 1935, King Reza Shah Pahlavi outlawed hijabs. Six years later, when his son took the throne, the new ruler gave women the freedom to wear or not wear the hijab based on personal choice. But as the Islamic Revolution gained steam and eventually overthrew the monarchy, the religious regime made women's modesty central to their control.[4] No longer a symbol of protest, the hijab became a symbol of conquest.

For the sake of their futures, young Iranian women are fighting back against the oppressive regime in the hopes of building a more just society. Iranian American journalist Imam Hariri-Kia explains in *The Cut*, "The protests are no longer centered around one incident, because the morality police are just the weapon being used to carry out a sentence, not the sentence itself. Iranians won't be satisfied with only getting rid of the force and compulsory hijab laws; they are leading a revolution, committed to fighting for democracy and basic human rights." Hariri-Kia goes on to say, "People tired of being mistreated and oppressed by the regime are doing whatever they can to destabilize it."[5]

In solidarity with Shiphrah and Puah, uncertainty of an outcome should never deter us from pursuing the next right choice, yet fear of consequences can give us pause. We'd like assurance of safety and fairness before we act, but no such promises are made. Queen Esther defied the law of the land when she appeared before the king unannounced, risking her life to do so. Rosa Parks defied Alabama state law when she refused to give up her seat. Their righteous defiance came with risk, but they both set in motion uprisings against injustice.

When weighing the possible cost of defiance, we must ask ourselves some questions: To whom does our allegiance belong? Is it to the world? The state? Our flesh? As followers of Jesus, we're regularly provided opportunities to acknowledge what and who we honor with our action or inaction, our obedience or disobedience. Kelley Nikondeha speaks to the midwives' loyalties in her book *Defiant*. She shares, "In their hierarchy of fears, it is God who most energizes them toward obedience amid dangerous times. Marshaling all their skill, they organize against death. They demonstrate a nervy faith that challenges us to do the same."[6] Like the midwives, many of us find ourselves in situations where our loyalty to institutions, or people, might be at odds with our convictions. In those moments, we must strive to act in accordance with our evolving faith, making decisions that honor our personhood and the dignity of others.

PRAYER

God of Shiphrah and Puah,
help me to stand for safety and care.
God of Renewal,
may my righteous defiance usher in justice.

• • •

DECLARATION

I will embrace the tension of defiance and duty.
May my voice and actions bend
the universe toward justice.

• • •

QUESTIONS TO PONDER

- Can you give another example of righteous defiance carried out in the interest of the dignity of humanity?
- Can you imagine an act of defiance of your own that would bend the universe toward justice?

30

Steadfast Joy

Let your hope keep you joyful, be patient in your troubles, and pray at all times.

—Romans 12:12 (GNT)

The practice of joy might seem a flowery outlier among other formative practices for renewal, such as defiance or humility. It might sound like a lightweight prospect when we think of which items in our home do or do not spark joy. Unlike happiness, joy is a response to the presence of the Divine not impeded by the constraints of life. It isn't frivolous, on the sidelines of our formation, but rather an emotional state we choose to embrace or decline. Romans 15:13 declares, "May the God of hope fill you with all joy and peace as you trust in him, so that you may overflow with hope by the power of the Holy Spirit." Jesus came so that we may boast in the full measure of his joy (John 17:13), and the joy of what was yet to come allowed him to endure the cross (Heb. 12:2). Nehemiah claimed, "The joy of the LORD is [our] strength" (Neh. 8:10). The Hebrew word for strength, *ma'owz*, assumes a place of safety, protection, or refuge.[1] Joy is a much-needed shelter, a gift of utility. The development of steadfast joy allows us to withstand the unthinkable, testifies to the presence of God, and clarifies our hopes and values.

Many of the original recipients of Scripture's instruction on practicing joy utilized this formative practice amid war, famine, and loss. They weren't strangers to joy under duress.

Kateri Tekakwitha, who came to be known as the Lily of the Mohawks,[2] knew the steadfast joy that the saints spoke of; she found it tucked in the presence of God. Kateri was orphaned at the age of five when a smallpox epidemic swept through her village and was raised by her relatives in Caughnawaga, along the Mohawk River in the 1660s, well before the state of New York was established. She remembered her parents fondly; her father was a tribal chief and her mother an Algonquin Catholic. Although Kateri survived the devastating outbreak, it left her vision impaired and her face scarred. Despite her poor vision, she became an excellent bead worker. Alongside others in her community, she farmed, fished, and harvested, all while embracing a vision of God as the creator of the natural world.

In her teen years, she was fascinated by stories of Jesus, and at twenty she was baptized. She reveled in her communion with the Divine among the trees and animals, but not everyone appreciated her strong faith. She refused to work on Sundays, and she would not marry the man her family chose for her. This led to hostility, threats of death, and her eventual escape on foot to a mission for Indigenous Catholics two hundred miles away near Montreal. Her desire for the presence of God superseded all else.

Kateri fused her indigenous values, which prioritized care for the natural world, with her growing faith and would later be known as the patron saint of traditional ecology. Those who knew her were fascinated by her quick wit and compassion as she taught the poor, young, and sick in her community. "They enjoyed being with her because they felt the presence of God. One time a priest asked the people why they gathered around Kateri in church. They responded that they felt close to God when Kateri prayed. They said that her face changed when she was praying; it became full of beauty and peace, as if she were looking at God's face."[3] Others found joy imitating her practice of pursuing the presence of God.

Although Kateri's life was cut short when she died in 1680 at the age of twenty-four, she would be forever remembered as one who found great joy in the presence of the Divine, often spending hours in prayer outdoors during cold Canada winters at a makeshift chapel she arranged in the woods. More than three hundred years after her death, in 2012, Kateri was canonized by Pope Benedict XVI.[4]

Despite the adversity of worsening health during the prime of her life and her estrangement from her extended family and larger community, Kateri knew the deep abiding joy that pays no mind to variables.

Joy thrives in good times and in bad. Barbara Brown Taylor writes, "Joy has never had very much to do with what is going on in the world at the time. This is what makes it different from happiness, or pleasure, or fun. All those depend on positive conditions. . . . The only condition for joy is the presence of God, . . . which means that it can erupt in a depressed economy, in the middle of a war, or in an intensive care waiting room. . . . It is a gift."[5] James 1:2 adds additional context to the nature of joy: "Consider it pure joy, my brothers and sisters, whenever you face trials of many kinds." Most of us would argue that trials do not equate to any measure of joy, but perhaps steadfast joy is at its juiciest, as an attribute of the Spirit's fruit, on our darkest days. Joy is not subject to factors outside our control; it is available in good times and bad. Joy is ours to cultivate. In trying times, it may feel irreverent or even indulgent to hold tight to joy, but it's sacred, a spiritual discipline. Joy has sustained our mothers and sisters across the world; it will sustain us too. Come what may.

PRAYER

God of St. Kateri,
may your joy be my strength.
Giver of Joy,
make me more like you.

• • •

DECLARATION

The presence of God goes before me,
enabling a spirit of steadfast joy.

QUESTIONS TO PONDER

- How does Jesus's commitment to the joy set before him encourage you in your season?
- How do you express joy in this season of life?

31

Carry One Another

Carry each other's burdens, and in this way you will fulfill the law of Christ.

—Galatians 6:2

While much of our spiritual formation is shaped by solitary disciplines, we care for ourselves and bring about social renewal when we humbly heal with women who love us. When we carry their burdens and they carry ours, we bring heaven to earth and fulfill the law of Christ. Our lives are made whole together.

The widows of India know that when we ache together, we can heal together.

When an Indian man's wife dies, he is expected to lead an ascetic life, but it's acceptable if he chooses to remarry. Grievously, if an Indian woman's husband passes away, these widows often face cruel abuse. As patrilineal custom dictates, brides leave their family and join their husband's family when they marry, often losing close connection with their blood relatives and subject to the whims of new relatives. When the unthinkable happens and they lose their partner, these women are viewed as liabilities by family members who feel no close connection to them. Many are shamed, starved, beaten, and locked away by their kin. Their savings are drained. Their social value is tanked. Their presence is considered bad luck. In conservative Hindu culture, wives aren't worthy of living if they can't retain the souls of their husbands.[1]

Many of these widows are illiterate, pledged at birth and married off young, and they end up on the streets if their family throws them out. Their widowed status disqualifies them from remarriage.[2] When misogynistic beliefs destroy their personhood, this is a clear example of how patriarchy can reduce a woman to nothing. And the problem is growing. Indian widows make up 10 percent of India's total population; that's more than forty million women, ranging in age from seven to ninety-seven.[3] They're castaways left to fend for themselves.

In years past, widows were expected to immolate themselves and lie beside their deceased husbands as the funeral pyres were set ablaze. While this practice has been banned since 1829, it has been replaced with widows enduring social and familial death. Jean Chapman notes, "Widows are expected to shed all physical adornments, including long hair, shave their heads, wear coarse white saris, and desist from wearing jewelry and makeup. There is a taboo for placing the red dot in the middle of the forehead denoting sexual energy. Widows are effectively de-sexualised, de-feminized, and uglified."[4] Many widows in North India make the trek to Vrindavan, a city south of New Delhi, to pray before the statues of the god Krishna in local temples. Widows began fleeing to Vrindavan after a sixteenth-century social reformer led a group of widows there to escape immolation. In their colorless saris, they beg and sing in the temples for rupees.[5] Some offer their bodies to religious pilgrims in hopes of earning income. Their profits line the pockets of local landlords who allow them to congregate, beg, and pray.[6] Forsaken by their families and considered useless to society, these beloved image bearers have been humbled through no fault of their own.

In a positive turn of events, in 2012 the Supreme Court of India passed measures funding programs to care for widows. Nonprofit groups and government organizations have created *vidhwa ashrams* (group homes for widows). Dotted along the countryside, these ashrams welcome widows to care for one another in the winter of their lives. They often arrive battered and without a rupee to their name. In these ashrams, they comfort each other in group therapy, sharing their stories of betrayal and loss, recognizing they aren't alone. Others understand and share their grief. They might dance through the halls on festival days, reclaiming simple joys stolen after their husbands passed. They might learn alongside each other to write their names, celebrating those who've mastered the skill. Over time, many have shed their white saris for colorful ones. They've traded their crying for laughter.[7] Their heaviness for joy. Their humble beginnings for humble endings. Together.

During the years many of us hope to dote on kids and grandkids and grow old with our spouses, the widows have exchanged their social shame for authentic connection with each other. They bear one another's burdens and care for one another. This is all they have, the treasure of each other, and they're living into a practice we can all glean from.

In *Braving the Wilderness*, Brené Brown answers the question of how we can grow together with this insight: "Show up for collective moments of joy and pain so we can actually bear witness to inextricable human connection. Women and men with the strongest true belonging practices maintain their belief in inextricable connection by engaging in moments of joy and pain."[8] Although we live in a highlight-reel era, sharing our vulnerable distress *and* private victories with those we trust allows us to treasure God's comfort and celebrate through and with others. Without safe women to build—or rebuild—our lives with, we may experience the silence of memory, with no one to remember and hold our stories. We are left feeling incomplete, undone.[9] Maya Angelou said it best in *I Know Why the Caged Bird Sings*: "There is no greater agony than bearing an untold story inside of you."[10] But we do not need to remain trapped in private pain with no one to light a candle in the dark of our distress. The widows know this to be true.

Vulnerability expressed in a safe space makes for a culture of cathartic healing, a true antidote for loneliness. Simply by allowing our stories to be acknowledged, we offer others the opportunity to care for us. Side by side, we inch toward joy and reimagine what life can look like after loss. Not a single soul is promised a cushy income, loving children, or beach vacations in the winter of our lives, but we can bear each other's burdens and so become like Christ to one another.

PRAYER

God of India's Widows,
be near me in humbling seasons.
God of My Winter,
give me companions for the journey.

• • •

DECLARATION

Among safe women, I can share my joy
and pain because I am known.
I will empathetically carry others' burdens
and so fulfill the law of Christ.

• • •

QUESTIONS TO PONDER

- In your humbling seasons, how have others modeled the empathy of Christ toward you?
- How can you model the empathy of Christ toward others?

32

Bearing Witness

She said to Jesus, "You are a Jew, and I am a Samaritan woman. Why are you asking me for a drink?"

—John 4:9 (NLT)

In our era of defensiveness, it's sacred to bear witness, to give what we have and kindly offer what we know. It's not just a gift to another but a gift to ourselves. Our anxieties, many of them triggered by socioeconomic and geopolitical obstacles, keep us on guard, hypervigilant to real or perceived threats. We're quick to hunker down in ideological bunkers and to set up guardrails against others who don't believe what we believe or act as we do. Reductively, we identify the "other" by every way in which they *aren't* like us, robbing them of their humanity along the way. Crouching in these bunkers, with walls built thick to keep others out, we forget how desperately we need to bear witness to one another—especially those who aren't like us but who may have something of value to teach us.

Breaking down these barriers might be one of the best decisions we ever make. It was for the Samaritan woman.

At Jacob's well in Sychar, the Samaritan woman bore witness to a kind, thirsty rabbi. Sychar was a place of meaning long before she arrived, with a storied past for the patriarchs of the Jewish faith. Some scholars suggest that this was where Abram settled after leaving his hometown of Haran (Gen. 12:6), where Jacob and his family returned after he dealt with his crooked father-in-law Laban (Gen. 33:18), where Jacob's daughter Dinah was assaulted (Gen. 34), and where Joseph's bones were buried (Josh. 24:32). For the Samaritan woman at the sweltering noon hour, Jacob's well in Sychar was a quiet place where she could fetch her daily water.

That was what she was doing when the weary rabbi approached her and struck up a conversation. She knew he was Jewish, a holy man, and she couldn't understand why he would share his very human need with her. In that time, it was culturally unacceptable for a rabbi to speak to a woman in public, even to his wife. Speaking to an unknown woman from Jewish-despised Samaria with a request to share her utensils was unheard of in the first century. Samaritans were considered half-breeds, an amalgamation of low-class Jewish peasants, conquered but not deported, who subsequently intermarried with the colonizing Assyrians (722 BC) and Babylonians (586 BC). In the eyes of devout Jews, their religious and ethnic identity was worse even than that of the unclean gentiles.

Yet Jesus, weary and worn down, exposes his humanity—and then his divinity—to this woman from a seemingly compromised background. This woman is often introduced in sermons and studies with commentary on all that she lost and who she shared a bed with, but Jesus begins a conversation by placing himself in her potential debt with a request for water. At Jacob's well, he is at the mercy of a woman he came to serve.[1] Further, archbishop of Constantinople John Chrysostom remarked that she didn't ridicule Jesus for his explanation of living water but spoke to him with kindness, patience, and curiosity.[2] It was no accident that his first acknowledgment of his true nature was to *her*. His transformative message wasn't limited to the Jews or to the gentiles but was true as well for this mixed-race Samaritan woman. One commentator notes, "In the meeting with the Samaritan woman at the well, John showed us Jesus has something to say to those despised by the religious establishment."[3] Notably, his disciples hadn't yet caught on to the full picture of Jesus's true identity, but the Samaritan woman did. She bore witness to his testimony and boldly shared the story that was still being written. Through her, the Samaritan townspeople entertained the claims of a Jewish foreigner.

In the account of Jesus and the Samaritan woman, we witness social, ethnic, and national boundary crossing, the sharing of vulnerable truth, and then, against the odds, fellow Samaritans welcoming a Jewish man into their community based on *her* enthusiastic response. Rose Mukansengimana-Nyirimana and Jonathan Draper remark, "After being challenged by Jesus' initial transcendence of the barriers caused by the existing social traditions, the transformed woman became a tool for unity building between the Judeans and the Samaritans. Understood from this perspective, the Samaritan woman becomes a mirror for and a challenge to women finding themselves in society marred with divisions, exclusion, and prejudice."[4] Her legacy doesn't stop there. Medieval hagiographers claim the woman's bold witness led to eventual martyrdom. Gothic lore claims she converted Nero's daughter in Rome, and another source claims she was imprisoned in Carthage for preaching the gospel.[5] By bearing witness to Jesus, the Samaritan woman became a peacemaker for estranged neighboring nations and stands as an exemplar that we can move toward unity with those unlike us, if only we proceed with the eyes and knowledge of Christ.

In our own fraught time, we can cross ethnic, spiritual, and gender barriers to walk alongside people different from us and, in the process, become fully ourselves. And who knows what the ripple effect might be hundreds of years after our passing if we are formed into people of peace, able to lay down our differences and to connect with others in the name of love—all while staying rooted in the way of the Divine. As we bear the image of God and bear witness to others, we'll be humbled by the holy in them as we discover the imprint of the Divine on their lives. Like the Samaritan woman, we'll find our place in the great gospel story; that's good news for women the world over.

PRAYER

God of the Samaritan Woman,
I welcome opportunity to bear witness to another.
Giver of Peace,
provide me understanding of others where I lack it.

● ● ●

DECLARATION

I am a peacemaker for the way
of love and connection.
Even when there is disagreement, I will
dignify those who are different from me.

● ● ●

QUESTIONS TO PONDER

- What ideological bunkers have been handed down to you?
- How do you reconcile your political and ethnic identity with your identity as a follower of Jesus?

PART 5

FUTURE LIBERATION

The greatest challenge of the day is: how to bring about a revolution of the heart, a revolution which has to start with each one of us.

—Dorothy Day

33

Arrival

Nevertheless, each person should live as a believer in whatever situation the Lord has assigned to them, just as God has called them.

—1 Corinthians 7:17

We rob ourselves of flourishing when we believe the lie that we have "made it" when we have money in the bank, a partner, children, a coveted promotion, a nice house, and everything that goes with it. Social media exacerbates this "if only" belief with a steady stream of highlight reels and success stories. With other people's victories buzzing in the back of our minds, we wonder when it might be our turn. When will we finally arrive? When will we make that much money? When will we find a partner? When will it all work out for us? Unsurprisingly, if we're convinced we've "arrived" when we've reached self-constructed milestones or achievements, then it's easy to move the target farther away the closer we inch toward it. Flourishing always seems just out of reach.

Phillis Wheatley was kidnapped from West Africa as a young child, probably around the age of seven, and was brought to Boston, where she was sold below market rate because she was deemed too young and frail for hard labor. The ship was bound for the southern colonies, but the captain was convinced that Phillis was ill and wished to profit off her before she died. Upon arrival in the harbor, she was bought by Susanna Wheatley, wife of a prominent businessman, and assigned to be her domestic housemaid. The Wheatleys named her Phillis after the ship on which she had been imprisoned and brought across the Atlantic, and they gave her their surname—a common practice during the colonial era. A relative of the family noted of the weary child that she was "of slender frame and evidently suffering from a change of climate . . . no other covering than a quantity of dirty carpet about her."[1] Stripped from the comfort of her home and country, transported inhumanely across the ocean, forced to learn a new language, and given a new name, Phillis was robbed of the life she deserved. Still, she never let others determine who she could be.

As the Wheatleys discovered Phillis's eager spirit to learn, they allowed their children, Mary and Nathaniel, to teach her how to read and write—a pursuit outlawed in southern colonies. While she was forced to serve them, she also chose to learn from them. She learned Scripture, geography, history, and literature. By age twelve, she read Greek and Latin classics in their original languages.[2] When she tried her hand at poetry, it was kismet. She gave herself to rhyme and never looked back. The Wheatley family was convinced Phillis's work was world class; the world certainly took note after she wrote an elegy for the famed preacher George Whitefield. Her poem, printed alongside the funeral sermon, earned her acclaim on both sides of the Atlantic. She was a prodigy, she knew it, and it was only the beginning.

Phillis sought out publishing opportunities and ran ads for subscribers in the Boston area newspapers but came up short. She was hard-pressed to find a publisher that would give a platform to an enslaved woman, but she persisted. She sent a collection of poems across the pond to Selina Hastings, Countess of Huntingdon. Selina was a prominent player in the eighteenth-century evangelical revivals, financing the movement and training ministers with her considerable fortune—especially those supporting abolitionist causes.[3] Before he passed, Whitefield had been Selina's chaplain, and she would have been familiar with Phillis's elegy. After receiving Phillis's request for assistance in getting her work published, Selina arranged for the British bookseller Archibald Bell to print her work. When Phillis arrived in Britain to finalize her manuscript, she was welcomed by British dignitaries and abolitionists—even Benjamin Franklin was among those who celebrated the gifted poetess. By the time she went back to Boston, Archibald Bell had released *Poems on Various Subjects, Religious and Moral*, the first book of poetry published by a Black woman in the modern era.

Unafraid to shy away from issues of her day, Phillis boldly applied biblical themes in her commentary on modern slavery. Her well-known poem "On Being Brought from Africa to America" implored White Christians to acknowledge and accept Africans within the faith, because the African men and women of faith knew they belonged. She reminded the White church:

> Remember, Christians, Negros, black as Cain,
> May be refin'd, and join th' angelic train.[4]

With clarity of mind and the power of the pen, Phillis continued to write poems that criticized the treatment of African Americans, advocating for an America that valued all its people and upheld the goodness of God. As an enslaved person in the eighteenth century, Phillis deserved freedom and full bodily autonomy but did not wait around for others to value her before pursuing the fullest version of herself.

Our flourishing is a daily event and won't look a lick like anyone else's. And it shouldn't. None of us exist to be a carbon copy of another; rather, each of us is a beloved image bearer pursuing the rich work of becoming fully ourselves, a recipient and conduit of God's grace and faithfulness. We'd be wise to recognize how we've been shaped and conditioned by the dreams America sold us, what others expect of us, and what society demands of us. We should not see ourselves—our gifts, our skills, our experiences, our resources—as being defined by everyone else except us. Phillis knew this. She wasn't waiting for permission to be known as more than an enslaved girl. She wasn't waiting to arrive, she already had—from her first breath until her last. A similar sensibility is echoed in the prayer of St. Theresa:

> *May today there be peace within you.*
> *May you trust God that you are exactly where you*
>   *are meant to be.*

*May you not forget the infinite possibilities that
    are born in faith.*
*May you use those gifts that you have received,
    and pass on the love that has been given to you.*
*May you be content knowing you are a child of
    God. Let this presence settle into your bones and
    allow your soul the freedom to sing, dance, praise
    and love. It is there for each and every one of us.*
Amen.[5]

A sense of arrival does not require that we compare ourselves to others or give up because flourishing feels out of reach. We are not late to our own lives. We trod on the path that's already been forged for us by the Divine, and at the same time we push for communal justice. We don't strive to arrive; we acknowledge we already have—and everyone else needs to keep up.

PRAYER

God of Phillis Wheatley,
give me energy to live fully without
permission from others.
God of Our Numbered Days,
show me yourself in every season.

• • •

DECLARATION

I am more than what others assume I am.
I have arrived at my one beautiful life.

QUESTIONS TO PONDER

- Have you felt late to your own life?
- Define in your own words a sense of arrival.

34

We Go High

> We continue to shout our praise even when we're hemmed in with troubles, because we know how troubles can develop passionate patience in us, and how that patience in turn forges the tempered steel of virtue, keeping us alert for whatever God will do next.
>
> —Romans 5:3–5 (Message)

As we're pursuing the fullness of Christ, the fruit of the Spirit proves necessary in times of conflict. With emotions running high, peace can quell the storm within us and patience can calm the storm around us. When the stakes are high, we can practice de-escalation—diffusing a tense encounter to prevent outrage or violence—centering connection, acknowledging vulnerabilities, and envisioning an alternative route. If we're hoping to usher in goodness and restoration, we'll need to reimagine a way forward forged by patience.

Abigail knew this to be true.

Married to boorish Nabal, Abigail intervenes when her husband ignores David's petition for food and shelter after the future king and his ragtag rebels set up camp on Nabal's land—offering protection for his livestock and those who are tending them. Word has spread that David is a formidable warrior, anointed future king of Israel, yet Nabal pays no mind to David, saying to his messengers, "Who is David? And who is the son of Jesse? There are many servants today who are each breaking away from his master. Shall I then take my bread and my water and my meat that I have slaughtered for my shearers, and give it to men whose origin I do not know?" (1 Sam. 25:10–11 NASB). Sick burn aside, Nabal's shortsighted response will be the beginning of his end.

David reacts by telling his men to prepare for slaughter. Warned by her servant of the impending massacre, Abigail jumps into action, ensuring her household and her people a future through regional peacekeeping. For David and his men, she packs an abundance of bread, wine, dressed sheep, roasted grain, and raisin and fig cakes. She loads them onto donkeys and follows behind. When she meets David and his four hundred men in a mountain ravine, they are already en route to annihilate every male under Nabal's rule. Wisely, she keeps her selfish husband in the dark while she diplomatically approaches David. Appealing to his better judgment, she agrees with David that her husband was foolish and explains that she didn't witness the exchange between David's messenger and Nabal. By appeasing David, Abigail prevents bloodshed. She offers her praise and provisions in gratitude to atone for Nabal's lack of hospitality. But she doesn't stop there.

Keenly reading the room, she prophesies that David will have a lasting dynasty as the appointed ruler of Israel. Despite others attempting to kill him, she tells him he will prevail because God is with him. Upon her return home, Abigail finds her husband drunk at his own party. She shrewdly chooses to wait until the morning to tell Nabal of her actions to protect him and his household. Stricken with fright or fury, he dies within a handful of days, but not at the hands of David. David tells Abigail at their mountainside meeting, "Blessed be the LORD God of Israel, who sent you this day to meet me, and blessed be your discernment, and blessed be you, who have kept me this day from bloodshed and from avenging myself by my own hand. Nevertheless, as the LORD God of Israel lives, who has restrained me from harming you, if you had not come quickly to meet me, there certainly would not have been left to Nabal until the morning light as much as one male" (1 Sam. 25:32–34 NASB). Without a doubt, David was grateful for the intervention, because if Abigail hadn't gone high, he would have gone very low.

In the Midrash, Abigail is known as one of seven female prophets, alongside Miriam, Deborah, Hannah, Sarah, Huldah, and Esther.[1] Like the others, she was capable of assessing the needs of the moment and strategically managing the issues at hand. Every single one of them could have reacted differently given their trying situations, but instead, their faith grounded them, and they conducted themselves with honor and valor in a time when women's lives were disposable. Dutch theologian Abraham Kuyper says of Abigail that she had "a most appealing character and unwavering faith."[2] In 1 Samuel 25, she not only delicately prevents a blood-bath but also ensures her own safety in the process—fusing resistance, generosity, and empathy for the sake of the future. Her character carries her through the toughest of situations.

In 2016, when first lady Michelle Obama uttered the words "When they go low, we go high," she likely had no idea that this phrase would resonate with the American public. Unpacking the short instruction to *Time* magazine, Mrs. Obama explained, "'Going high' doesn't mean you don't feel the hurt, or you're not en-titled to an emotion. It means that your response has to reflect the solution. It shouldn't come from a place of anger or vengefulness." She added, "When I say, 'go high,' I'm not trying to win the argument. I'm trying to figure out how to understand you and how I can help you understand me."[3] Legions of women caught in seemingly lose-lose situations have sought to learn of the motivations, losses, and hurts of those who don't see them with the same patience and poise as Abigail. They've sought to find a third way, a solution for the complicated moments without giving in to rage or fear.

Like those who've gone before us, we can profess our rage without allowing it to blind us and get the better of us as David almost did. Rather, in pursuit of future liberation, we move from anger to acknowledgment to accurately ascertain how we can address the injustice. We can make room for the fruit of the Spirit to blos-som where it's needed most. When we've been served volatility, we offer peace and patience. When we've been saddled with disrespect, we offer kindness and good-ness. When we've been disgraced by those who don't see us, we respond with gentleness and self-control. In the way of the upside-down kingdom, we're healed by the nourishing fruit of the Spirit in us and through us, again and again.

PRAYER

God of Abigail,
help me to fuse my resistance with
generosity and empathy.
God of Peace and Patience,
give me the wisdom to assess
the needs of the moment.

• • •

DECLARATION

I'll go high,
no matter how humbling the moment.

• • •

QUESTIONS TO PONDER

• How can you move from anger to acknowledgment in moments of tension?
• In what current situations do you hope to nourish others by the fruit of the Spirit?

35

The Future Belongs to Us

PRICELIS PERREAUX-DOMINGUEZ

And who knows but that you have come to your royal position for such a time as this?

—Esther 4:14

Ensuring a future of flourishing might mean diplomatically petitioning your husband-king to spare your people, as was the case with Esther; for other women, it may mean clearing the dinner table in order to assemble weapons to fight an evil dictator. A peaceful future requires all kinds of actions and all kinds of women.

In the 1940s, three sisters, known as las hermanas Mirabal, lived under the dictatorship of Rafael Trujillo in the Dominican Republic. In the late years of his dictatorship, las hermanas Mirabal made their mark, but before I say more about them, let me tell you a little bit more about the setting and tone of the Dominican Republic in the time of Trujillo.

The Dominican Republic is the only island in the Caribbean that shares its land with another country—Haiti—and most of the people there speak Spanish. It has a history of oppression under various colonizers, including Spain, France, and Great Britain. The people are mainly of African, Arab, and European descent. On top of this, it's also a place where women have been highly oppressed, marginalized, and othered—as in many other countries around the world.

Dictators can assert authority in many different ways, and Rafael Trujillo believed himself to be a kind of god. Many Dominicans had a picture of White Jesus on the wall in their home, and Trujillo required the occupants to replace that with a picture of him. If they dared to refuse, they risked being arrested or killed. In his early years as dictator, he led the Parsley Massacre, which included the slaughter of more than twenty thousand Haitians. Las hermanas Mirabal, also known as las Mariposas (in English, the butterflies), were women who created an underground movement to stop Trujillo. The resistance was led by the sisters, their husbands, and a community of activists who loved their country and wanted to return dignity to their people.

Perhaps this story sounds familiar. Have you read the book of Esther? Sometimes we focus so much on certain parts of this narrative that we miss the broader storyline and message. There, we see two versions of Trujillo: King Xerxes of Persia and his adviser, Haman. They are the two men in charge, and both use their power for oppression, rule-setting, and self-aggrandizement.

King Xerxes held a banquet that lasted a hundred days in celebration of his rule and his glory—which sounds similar to how Trujillo wanted a picture of himself in each Dominican home.

We can look back and see numerous examples throughout history of how an evil power player reigned but eventually succumbed through the actions of courageous individuals like Esther and las hermanas Mirabal. We see it with Jesus on the cross, we see it with Harriet Tubman and the Underground Railroad, we see it in revolution after revolution, and we see it still today—because of people who strive for dignity to triumph over dehumanization, not just for the redemption of what happened in the past but for renewal in the present and a deep restorative hope for the future.

Because of Esther and Mordecai's commitment to dignity and freedom, the Jews were not killed.

Because of las hermanas Mirabal's commitment to dignity and freedom, people rose up and overthrew Trujillo's tyrannical dictatorship, and the Dominican people forged a new path forward.

History teaches us over and over that hope for the future isn't a foolish notion but an essential vision to getting where God is taking us, but our present work is what makes the real impact.

This is why the future belongs to us; we are the ones shaping it right now with each decision, thought, word, contribution, sacrifice, prayer, and commitment.

As a society, we are surrounded by people like Haman, Xerxes, and Trujillo. But there are plenty of Esthers and Butterflies who can shape our future as well.

One of the motivating factors for many things we do in life is being able to see the results, but much of the impact of our efforts now may not be immediately apparent but will bear fruit in the future. Our small seeds form not just future decades but future centuries. Our fight and fervor produce fruit that will guide generations years from now, hopefully in the interest of justice, dignity, and goodness, as did the fight and fervor of our cohorts Esther and the Butterfly Sisters.

Every year, the Jewish community celebrates Purim, a holiday that began in the time of Esther to remember her obedience and God's goodness. November 25 marks the International Day for the Elimination of Violence against Women, a day that began in honor of las hermanas Mirabal.

Your fight is not in vain.

This is why being alive right now in such a time as this is no accident.

The image bearer that you have been appointed to be right now is needed for the present and the future.

You may be reading this and thinking, "*That sounds nice, but that's not me.*" Friend, you have breath in your lungs; so yes, it is for you. Every living thing was created to give God praise, as seen in Psalm 150:6, and that praise happens through the everyday lived in obedience to God and our striving to fulfill God's good plan for us.

The future belongs to us because we are the ones obediently praising and fighting during the mundane and the miracles, standing up for justice through policymaking while also faithfully making our children meals each day, holding sacred spaces for the marginalized, and helping our literal neighbor be seen by learning their name. You may never be known by millions or have your story told in books like Esther and las hermanas Mirabal do, but beloved, your name is certainly written in a book. Philippians 4:3 reminds us that women were there from the beginning: "Yes, I ask you also, true companion, help these women, who have labored side by side with me in the gospel together with Clement and the rest of my fellow workers, whose names are in the book of life" (ESV). The apostle Paul wrote of women whose names can be found in the book of life.

We can join them.

We are alive and here for such a time as this, to live in contentment and beauty that exist because of those who came before us. While you get to enjoy the fruit of their sacrifices, you are also called to work in the present for the future. The future is a collective flourishing for the glory of God and the goodness that permeates earth and will come to pass by our lives well lived.

PRAYER

God of Las Hermanas Mirabal,
give me the boldness and clarity to
contribute nourishing fruit while I'm here.
God of Revolutionaries to Come,
lead my heart and hands today for
the greater good of tomorrow.

· · ·

DECLARATION

I will embrace the contribution I'm called
to make to this world at this time.
I will be a vessel for change while allowing
the Holy Spirit to give me boldness.

QUESTIONS TO PONDER

- How does your current place in life (income, location, privilege, or beliefs) allow you to be someone who plants seeds for the future?
- What consistent contribution can you make to the world for the glory of God and the good of others?

36

Consent to Reality

Forget about what's happened;
    don't keep going over old history.
Be alert, be present. I'm about to do
        something brand-new.
    It's bursting out! Don't you see it?
There it is! I'm making a road through the
        desert,
    rivers in the badlands.

—Isaiah 43:18 (Message)

What if we arrive to become the person we hoped to be, not because we avoided feelings of resentment but because we pulled them up by the roots? What if we attended to the tubers of anger and regret, shame and bitterness? How would that redefine our story? What if freedom from resentment lies in accepting our reality?

We are not always in control of what happens to us, but we are responsible for how we react to it.

During the Rwandan genocide, Immaculée Ilibagiza and seven other women held their breath and their hope as former friends with machetes raided their village. Together these women huddled in a tiny hidden bathroom for ninety-one days. Immaculée was a healthy, well-loved university student when she hunkered down in the bathroom, only to emerge three months later weighing sixty-five pounds. She soon learned her entire family had been slaughtered.[1] Through no fault of her own, she lost everything precious to her. She had every reason to let anger boil over to resentment, yet she sought another way.

Clutching the rosary beads her Catholic father had given her, Immaculée prayed from sunup to sundown; she did this not only because her body was trapped but also to keep her tortured mind from giving in to resentment for all she endured.[2] To drown out the rage, she sank into Scripture, repeating the Lord's Prayer until it was etched onto her soul. In her book *Left to Tell*, she writes, "I knew that my heart and mind would always be tempted to feel anger—to find blame and hate. But I resolved that when the negative feelings came upon me, I wouldn't wait for them to grow or fester. I would always turn immediately to the Source of all true power: I would turn to God and let His love and forgiveness protect and save me."[3] After months of mental, emotional, and physical suffering, she learned to live with her new reality, and when offered the opportunity to forgive her mother's murderer, she did. Immaculée went on to work for the United Nations, advocating for peace in war-torn places. Layli Maparyan notes in

The Womanist Idea that Immaculée's story is one of self-change paving the way for social change. She writes that "active self-reflection is the foundation of effective social transformational work."[4]

No matter our journey, moving from self-care to social renewal requires accepting our reality. We must work through our resentment, that sense that we're stuck with the short end of the stick—with notes of agony and disappointment that can feel nearly impossible to overcome. We mourn unfulfilled dreams and opportunities missed. Therapist Christiana Ibilola Awosan explains that resentment is "an intense, multi-layered emotion that has components of anger, bitterness, indignation, sadness, humiliation, and shame attached to it."[5] It leaves us brooding over what should have been. It's an unfortunate reminder that much of life is happening to us, and although we'd love to pull the strings, our well-being hinges on our responses to actions outside our control.

For those of us who start in life with limited options and few resources, our best choice might be another's last choice. If we've had caregivers who failed to meet our emotional and physical needs or were born into broken systems, it's devastating to realize how fractured our "normal" is. Additionally, if harm, neglect, or disrespect is the norm for us, we can miss the signposts on our journey that point the way to higher ground. We might find ourselves tossed into a vicious cycle of resentment for how we've been treated and the subsequent decisions we've made—despite doing our best.

Resentment might ask, "Where is God in all of this?" All the while, the Divine waits to tenderly exchange the weight of regrets and fantasies for freedom, an embodied knowledge of love and care that empowers us to accept the life we have and forgive those who've harmed us.

Yet it's distressing to arrive at a particular age and realize we harbor deep regret for where we are or who we are. The pain of choices made, or choices made for us, lingers in our brains days, months, and years after the fact.[6] It's easy to ruminate on what could have been, the life we could have had, the partner that got away, the risks we didn't take, the job we didn't quit, the baby we thought we'd have. It's soul-sucking.

Henri Nouwen, in *The Return of the Prodigal Son*, writes, "Resentment is an inner complaint. I discover within me that murmuring, whining, grumbling, lamenting, and griping that go on and on even against my will. The more I dwell on the matters in question, the worse my state becomes."[7] Unchecked, resentment leaves the door open for anxiety and depression over a past we can't alter.[8] And it paints others as the villain in our story when they are in need of divine healing just as much as we are. The well-being that resentment robs from us can be restored through acceptance. We witness this in the life of Joseph, when as governor of Egypt he declares to his brothers, "I am Joseph, your brother, whom you sold into slavery in Egypt. But don't be upset, and don't be angry with yourselves for selling me to this place. It was God who sent me here ahead of you to preserve your lives" (Gen. 45:4–5 NLT). Joseph accepted what had happened to him and did not let resentment eat away at him; instead, he chose to mine his past for lessons that helped him make sense of his presence.

When we arrive in a place of spiritual and psychological safety, we can process our experiences with unending grace and mercy. For Immaculée, when resentment crept up on her, she remembered her true source of comfort, and Joseph continued to turn to God after his brothers sold him into slavery. Both eventually forgave those who harmed them, the ones who robbed them of what was precious to them. Resentment was exchanged for peace and forgiveness that surpasses understanding.

Far too many of us are experts at suppressing resentment, paving over it in hopes that it might disappear; instead, it blooms through the cracks of our days, reminding us that we can't escape ourselves or our stories. It's not a revisionist history we need, nor is blaming ourselves helpful. We need compassion for the woman we were, doing the best we could with the resources we had. We are beloved by the Divine, and that has not changed. Further, noting the goodness and renewal discovered in the wake of injustices heaped on us as we walk in the fullness of Christ attunes the eyes of our heart to pay attention to the hand of the Divine. If we consent to our current reality, we strip off the weight of resentment that slows us down in the race set before us and set the pace for others to go and do likewise.

PRAYER

God of Immaculée,
remove from me the weight of resentment.
Healer of Our Days,
ground me as I live into my renewal story.

DECLARATION

I consent to reality,
because I know you're with me.

• • •

QUESTIONS TO PONDER

- Has resentment sullied your ability to enjoy the sweet moments of this season?
- As thoughts of resentment burn in your mind, how can you react with gentleness toward yourself?

37

Hospitality amid Hostility

What good is it, my brothers and sisters, if someone claims to have faith but does not have works? Can this kind of faith save him? If a brother or sister is poorly clothed and lacks daily food, and one of you says to them, "Go in peace, keep warm and eat well," but you do not give them what the body needs, what good is it? So also faith, if it does not have works, is dead being by itself.

—James 2:14–17 (NET)

Extending hospitality in an inhospitable world is an act of liberation. Acts of kindness in the face of cruelty keep us attuned to the needs of others and our souls. We carve out space for others to find their selves in the story of goodness and renewal as the hospitable God makes a home in us.

In January 1969, at the request of Father Earl Neil, Ruth Beckford-Smith of St. Augustine's Church in Oakland, California, recruited neighborhood mamas to serve breakfast to hungry Black children who often went to school with grumbling bellies, making it nearly impossible for them to stay focused and learn. An effort sponsored by the Black Panthers, free breakfast for community children would address gaps in social care unmet by local schools. Local businesses, churches, and organizations gifted space for the program and nourishing donations of eggs, grits, toast, and milk. Other mamas around the country were encouraged to do the same, and they fed more than twenty thousand children nationally in 1969, with twenty-six cities participating. In a US Senate hearing the same year, the National School Lunch Program administrator determined that the Black Panther mamas at St. Augustine's and other mamas like them fed more poor school students than the State of California.[1]

FBI director J. Edgar Hoover took note of the breakfast program's tremendous achievements and deemed the Panthers "the greatest threat to the internal security of the country" due to their Free Breakfast Program.[2] Enraged that the program drew support from liberal Whites and moderate Black citizens, he vowed to destroy it. Hoover and his agents sent letters to stores and suppliers, discouraging them from donating; they spread gossip that the Panther mamas fed poisoned food to the children, and they raided sites while children ate. By the early seventies, many of the sites had closed. The last surviving site, in Seattle, shut down in 1977. Despite closures, program leaders urged Congress to address how they might care for the nation's poor and hungry children. By 1975, the Free Breakfast Program's emphasis on before-school meal service had pushed Congress to provide free breakfast nationwide for qualifying students in all public schools.[3] Today, in America's public schools, 11.8 million students who might otherwise go hungry receive a free breakfast.[4]

Neighborhood mothers put the US government to shame when it came to taking care of their little ones. When it came to hospitality, they knew what it looked like, what it tasted like, and how it could lift a community. Their ordinary contribution could bring heaven to earth. They provided hospitality to hungry bellies before six hours of math and reading. Detractors be damned. Setbacks only fueled their fire.

To give one example of the animosity they faced, the night before the Chicago breakfast site opened, police broke into the church and destroyed the food donated for the children by smashing the supplies and urinating all over them.[5] Delayed but undeterred, parishioners went out again, collecting donations in hopes of welcoming the little ones for breakfast. Those mamas set a table of hospitality in a country steeped in racism, classism, and sexism. They embodied the hospitable gospel to feed their communities. True hospitality grants belonging and the rights of a community to those who have been outside of it, to the vulnerable, the left behind, and those robbed of inclusion.

For those of us attempting to create a life and legacy in a system that was designed to exclude certain people from the table, it can feel daunting attempting to rebuild something we didn't break or to serve another what we were starved of. Positive change requires reparenting and reteaching ourselves our worth when we've been subjected to discrimination, harm, or neglect. Positive change asks us to enact boundaries, setting out clear delineations of what we will and won't accept. While we may have once been on the outside looking in, hoping for scraps, we're now setting up the chairs and laying the plates for all to feast at the table of renewal. In *Liberty and Freedom*, David Hackett Fisher notes that the word *free* descends from the Indo-European term *priya*, meaning "dear" or "beloved." He surmises, "Free meant someone who was joined to a tribe . . . by ties of kinship and rights of belonging."[6] Freedom was, and arguably is, connection by affection; it is an endeavor by the individual and the collective to flourish and achieve by caring for and belonging to one another. It's a return to what should be rather than accepting what is. It's creating space to restore others as we are being restored.

In the absence of hospitality we may be tempted to exclude or reject others, regurgitating our own negative experiences onto others. Cole Arthur Riley writes in *This Here Flesh*, "If you go without belonging for long enough, if you've known the sting of betrayal, you can end up manufacturing an identity from your alienation."[7] Ruth Beckford-Smith and the neighborhood mothers in Oakland knew the sting of rejection by a country that segregated and discriminated against them, and still, overflowing with the hospitable goodness of the gospel, they rewrote the book on hospitality. We can rewrite the book too. With that same hospitable Holy Spirit, we can set the table and invite all to dine. As we work, befriend, parent, lead, write, teach, listen, feed, and learn, we are healing. Every single day.

PRAYER

God of Ruth Beckford-Smith,
give me a vision to set the table for the hungry.
God of the Neighborhood Mothers,
allow my collective care to impact
generations upon generations.

• • •

DECLARATION

I will set a table for all to dine in peace,
serving refreshment as I am also renewed.

• • •

QUESTIONS TO PONDER

- How might you set a table for everyone?
- What does hospitality mean to you in this season?

38

Who Are We Becoming?

SARA SHABAN

You, my brothers and sisters, were called to be free. But do not use your freedom to indulge the flesh; rather, serve one another humbly in love. For the entire law is fulfilled in keeping this one command: "Love your neighbor as yourself."

—Galatians 5:13–14

To become the women we've been waiting for, we must humanize one another and recognize the dignity of every image bearer, no matter how different another woman is from us. We must forgo an "us versus them" mindset. Our formation depends on it.

In the early 1970s, Angela Davis took a trip to Egypt after being asked to write an article focused on women in another country during the United Nations' Decade for Women (1975–1985). Specifically, Angela was asked to write a piece on Egyptian women and sex, with an emphasis on female genital mutilation. Initially, she wasn't aware that this was the purpose of the trip and reconsidered going altogether; however, rather than backing out, she used this as an opportunity to engage with women in Egypt in a way that didn't focus on them as victims but as feminists seeking gender equality. In her book *Women, Culture, and Politics*, she writes:

> As an Afro-American woman familiar with the sometimes hidden dynamics of racism, I had previously questioned the myopic concentration on female circumcision in US feminist literature on African women. The insinuation seems frequently to be made that the women in the twenty or so countries where this outmoded and dangerous practice occurs would magically ascend to a state of equality once they managed to throw off the fetters of genital mutilation—or, rather, once white Western feminists (whose appeals often suggest that this is the contemporary "white women's burden") accomplished this for them. The dynamics here are not entirely dissimilar from those characterizing the historical campaign waged by US feminists for the right to birth control.[1]

Angela highlights the problematic framing of groups of women by other women who are *not* part of those communities.

Steering away from this approach, she drew parallels between Egyptian women and Afro-American women that remove the exoticism associated with Egypt and instead highlight its citizens as seeking gender equality just like women in the United States. The bridge of solidarity built here is what experts call transnational feminism.

The goal of news media is to help us make sense of world events. Inevitably, this can lead to stereotypes. Western media often has a confirmation bias when it comes to coverage of Muslim women, meaning they almost exclusively report on Muslim women through a victimizing lens and often out of context. Contrary to the way they are presented in American news coverage, Arab and Muslim women are no strangers to activism and social movements. History shows that throughout the Middle East and North Africa, women play a pivotal role in anti-imperialist causes and gender equality movements, bringing us to transnational feminism.

In a nutshell, transnational feminism rejects a single or universal form of feminism and, instead, engages in feminist practices within context: cultural, political, or geographical. Arab and Muslim women are often stereotyped as being forced to wear the burqa and the hijab, but every woman's experience is different. For instance, before 1979, the hijab was prohibited in Iran because the Shah believed the covering hindered the country's rise to modernity. Similarly, in France several mandates ban the hijab because some feel it interferes with the country's secular culture. However, in the United States many activists are working to normalize the hijab. Some companies are treating the covering as a commodity—like Macy's luxury hijab line and Nike's athletic hijabs. Some women choose to wear hijabs for political reasons rather than religious ones.

Western feminism often overemphasizes gender as the primary cause of women's oppression. This perspective has been used to justify war and colonization in the name of liberating women, especially in the Middle East. Specifically, Arab and Muslim women are characterized as oppressed, docile, uneducated, and sexualized—whether as jihadi brides or belly dancers. A lot of these stereotypes are perpetuated through films and TV shows. Those stereotypes set the stage for dangerous ideas, like femonationalism, which means using feminist and gender-equality language to promote anti-Islamic and xenophobic campaigns.[2]

For example, Afghan women and their bodies have long been manipulated to illustrate their otherness; their covered bodies are presented as a symbol of backwardness and oppression. The removal of the veil becomes a sign of modernity and liberty. From the beginning, the "war on terror" was unquestionably linked to liberating Afghan women. And this liberation came in the form of visual markers of *progress*. In many ways, this campaign to liberate Afghan women, which focused heavily on veiling, has endured, where Afghan women's bodies and clothing remain a central focus.

Afghan women are no strangers to the world of online activism, with the Revolutionary Association of the Women of Afghanistan (RAWA) launching a website in 1996. While Afghanistan had a high rate of illiteracy at the time of the launching of the website, RAWA's online content was not intended for a domestic audience but for an international one. The internet serves as a valuable space for marginalized groups to generate media attention outside of their local sphere of influence—aiming for international awareness. But those same connections can circulate problematic stereotypes, in this case of Afghan women.

The success of online movements is often dependent on transnational support, which can be difficult to sustain if the support group does not agree with the movement's understanding of feminism. While Western feminism has paraded stereotypes of oppressed, veiled Muslim women in their campaigns to "save" Afghan women, Afghan women may find themselves "playing to the camera" to attract the right audience: Westerners. Because Western feminism has historically latched on to "liberation" campaigns focused on the unveiling of Muslim women, Afghan women have used this understanding of feminism, highlighting their otherness to garner global attention. That's problematic.

So, what does that mean for us? Power structures often pit women against each other. These are narratives that tell women, "What are you complaining about? At least you don't have it as bad as *they* do," creating an "us versus them" scenario that assumes a "West is best" attitude. These narratives inform our assumptions about women we see in the supermarket, the ones driving down the road, and the ones we see on our screens. Those assumptions are based on what Chimamanda Ngozi Adichie refers to as "the danger of a single story."[3] The danger of a single story highlights the idea that complex people and situations can't be reduced to a single narrative. As much as we would like for things to be black and white, we have to embrace the gray. As a former journalist, I can say with confidence that there is a strong relationship between power and narrative. The stories we hear are not the only stories that exist.

As women, we are fighting not only against narratives that stereotype our culture or our faith but also against stereotypes that keep women in a box. We live in a world that highlights our differences, sometimes in good ways but often in damaging ones. There is a difference between appreciating our diversity and emphasizing deviations from whatever the standard happens to be at the time. Yet we modify our interpretations of the world depending on who we are in the moment. We spend a lot of time thinking about who we are and who others are, but we'd be wise to think about who we are becoming. Are we becoming women who support other women, or are we women who support the power structures that maintain an "us versus them" framework?

While norms and agendas may fluctuate, our God stays the same. The invitation remains as pertinent today as it was to women in the Galatian church: be free; don't indulge but rather serve in love. This is the way of the Lord.

PRAYER

God of All Cultures and People,
give me eyes to see and ears to listen.
God of My Becoming,
guide me as I evolve into a
woman of understanding.

• • •

DECLARATION

I am learning and will recognize
where I got it wrong.
I am continually becoming a woman
who supports other women.

QUESTIONS TO PONDER

- What assumptions do you have about the meaning of feminism?
- In what ways do you assume a "West is best" perspective?

39

Love Is the Final Fight

Love never gives up, never loses faith, is always hopeful,
and endures through every circumstance.

—1 Corinthians 13:7 (NLT)

The love that forms our souls and liberates us, that
defies the odds, has a measure of sacrifice baked into
our DNA.

Saul's concubine Rizpah, mentioned in 2 Samuel 21,
offers us what Donald Davidson calls a "pure white
shaft of sacrifice and love."[1] Rizpah held vigil over her
sons' slain bodies for months after they were ceremo-
nially executed by the Gibeonites. She "spread burlap
on a rock and stayed there the entire harvest season.
She prevented the scavenger birds from tearing at their
bodies during the day and stopped wild animals from
eating them at night" (v. 10 NLT). Their death was an
act of vengeance against their father, Saul, for invading

the land of the Gibeonites and slaughtering the people there, which ushered in a famine throughout Israel. To atone for Saul's actions, Israel allowed his heirs to be executed. They paid a debt for a crime they did not commit to restore tribal peace and end the famine. Rizpah's passionate, perseverant love for her sons could not keep them alive, but in their death she exercised her power the only way she could. She stayed with their bodies at the gallows until David agreed to allow them a proper burial alongside Saul and Jonathan. In her book *Womanist Midrash*, Wilda Gafney makes this observation: "Lynching Rizpah and Merab's sons did not heal the land or the people. Doing right by the multiply wronged women did."[2] Rizpah's enduring love unleashed justice not only for her but for a nation. Triumph began with a mother's fierce love.

In civil rights–era America, eighteen-year-old Mildred Loving was ripped out of her bed by law enforcement and locked in a jail cell without bail for three nights in Caroline County, Virginia. Her crime was her marriage to her White husband, Richard. After the lovebirds pled guilty for violating Virginia's Racial Integrity Act, they were given an ultimatum: go to prison or leave Virginia for twenty-five years. They left—sacrificing their way of life, jobs, family, and friends. After a class action lawsuit and a trip to the court of appeals, the Lovings took their case all the way to the Supreme Court. Their lawyers argued before the justices that their clients were denied due process and equal protection under the Fourteenth Amendment. Lo and behold, after the Lovings fought for nine years in the name of love, the court unanimously agreed, and the rights of those in interracial marriages were recognized nationwide.

Activist John Perkins claimed that "love is the final fight,"[3] and perhaps he's right. Love that perseveres and seeks to right wrongs is terrifying to unjust structures we've long accepted as normal. Love unmasks rules and rites steeped in prejudice and jealousy, hate and violence. Love is the legs of justice and dares to rewrite expectations that lean toward redemption and restoration. It defies the odds. First Corinthians 13:6–7 explains that love "does not rejoice about injustice but rejoices whenever the truth wins out. Love never gives up, never loses faith, is always hopeful, and endures through every circumstance" (NLT). An enduring love like Rizpah's or Mildred's is not limited by what may seem reasonable to others. Love doesn't quit, even if others have given up. Love never claims to measure itself against current trends. With their eyes fixed on justice in the name of love, these two women were unapologetic and tenacious in their approach. Cornel West says, "Justice is what love looks like in public."[4] We'll know it's the love Scripture describes because others are better for it. It's shaping others as much as it's shaping us.

Like the Divine's own enduring love, evidenced most dramatically in Christ's death and resurrection, love is both the driving force and the end goal—not only for the giver but for all. Sacrificial love liberates us and sets us free. We might wonder, "If love is so beautiful, so restorative in nature, why does it demand so much? Why does it hurt? If love is free, then why the steep cost?" Perhaps when we sacrifice we gain clarity, we gain momentum, we gain conviction to see love's purposes materialize. I imagine that months into Rizpah's vigil, she had as much resolve as she did on day one to see her sons properly buried. Mildred and Richard's fight to be recognized as a married couple took eight years of steadfast determination. Like Rizpah and Mildred, who both revered the Lord of Love, may we practice enduring love without reservation for the renewal of all.

PRAYER

God of Rizpah,
create in me a selfless heart.
God of Mildred,
grant me endurance through all circumstances.

• • •

DECLARATION

I am lovable as I am.
I love with intention and without reservation.

• • •

QUESTIONS TO PONDER

- Who have you withheld love from and why?
- In this season, who needs your patient and enduring love?

40

Becoming a Non-anxious Presence

Surely the righteous will never be shaken;
   they will be remembered forever.
They will have no fear of bad news;
   their hearts are steadfast, trusting in the
   LORD.

—Psalm 112:6–7

Responding to tragedy or disappointment is a part of life. Our time on earth will present us with countless situations in which we feel helpless, but even in the most chaotic times we can cultivate a non-anxious presence—unshaken and calm.

Poet and activist Sarojini Naidu, nicknamed the Nightingale of India, was appointed leader of the historic Salt March by Gandhi after he was arrested for nonviolent resistance against the British salt monopoly.[1] Originally, Gandhi had discouraged women from marching for fear of arrest and assault, but Sarojini and others convinced him that women's civil disobedience, their peaceable presence, was necessary to overthrow imperialistic Britain.[2] With the world watching, Sarojini calmly led twenty-five hundred marchers in the Salt Satyagraha,[3] where many would be attacked and beaten by police, but they remained peaceful.[4]

Throughout her life she embodied serenity in chaotic times. Dedicated to civil rights and women's emancipation by word and deed, Sarojini advocated for equality and peace in an increasingly anxious country. In 1925, she was elected the first female president of the Indian National Congress.[5] In 1947, when India finally gained independence from the British after eighty-nine years of rule, she was appointed governor of the United Provinces (modern-day Uttar Pradesh). As the first female governor of India, she faithfully served her people until her death at the age of seventy. Sarojini longed for Mother India to be a land of love, peace, and truth, and she embodied those virtues in her life and work. In one of her most well-known poems, "Song of a Dream," she wrote of a visionary land, depicting liberation as commonplace:

> Soul-deep in visions that poppy-like sprang;
> And spirits of Truth were the birds that sang,
> And spirits of Love were the stars that
>   glowed,
> And spirits of Peace were the streams that
>   flowed.[6]

Like Sarojini, Syrian sisters Sara and Yursa embodied a non-anxious presence when it was needed most. As they attempted to flee war-torn Syria in 2015, they boarded a boat with twenty others in Turkey and headed for Greece. Warned there was only a slim chance they'd reach their destination, they feared the worst when their engine gave out and the boat began to take on water. To save those on board, the sisters, both competitive swimmers, jumped into the water and pushed the boat through the night in chilly waters. Sara remarked of their feat, "I thought it was my duty to jump in the water. And if I die and those 20 people are still alive, that's great. When I die people would remember me for this. But if I leave them, I would feel bad with myself for the rest of my life." Their eyes clogged with salt water and fighting to stay awake, they eventually reached a Greek island. Sara admitted that she assumed if ever put in a situation of life or death, she'd try to save herself first, but when the most anxious of moments came along, "I felt that life was bigger than me alone. All the people on that boat were part of me."[7] Their non-anxious presence saved lives and led to liberation—their own included.

In *Generation to Generation*, Jewish therapist Edwin H. Friedman explains how any system, family, or community will fare poorly in times of chaos unless there is at least one person who models a non-anxious presence. To embody a non-anxious presence, he concludes that, first, one must intentionally choose to be holistically present within a crisis, and second, one must maintain calm in the midst of panic. Irrational actions or accusations are set aside in favor of peaceful solutions and problem-solving—allowing the steadfast spirit from within to permeate the presence of others. Referring specifically to the role of pastoral shepherds but applicable to all, he notes, "To the extent we function and grow within the context of our own souls (a lifetime project) and abet the emergence of our own selves (by a willingness to face life's challenges and oneself), our spirituality and our tradition will spring naturally from our being."[8] Our ability to partner with the Divine in communal renewal is largely determined by the health of our interior life. Who we have become and how we have nurtured ourselves is paramount when others' well-being is on the line. Consciously or unconsciously, we'll replicate what's buried within us. If we've been sown in the soil of healing, we'll reap a harvest of wholeness and goodness, nourishing those around us. This can be a tall order if trauma or loss, resentment or rage, is weaved within our stories. Yet this is the wonder of life in Christ, an exchange of beauty for ashes. A way through the darkness. A faithful companion for the journey.

When crashing waves surround us, our non-anxious presence by way of the Holy Spirit may be the proverbial lighthouse for others. We might be the ones to pick up the mantle of leadership under oppressive rule, the ones to kick to safety, the ones to shine in the moment with unshakable resolve. We may be terrified and tired, yet the image of God burns bright, refining our rough edges and assuring future liberation for all to come. It's in these moments, these chaotic times, that we recognize we are the women we've been waiting for. It was in us all along.

PRAYER

God of Sarojini,
may the Spirit of truth, love, and
peace flow from within me.
God of Sara and Yursa,
give me a holy resolve to remain non-
anxious in moments of chaos.

• • •

DECLARATION

I will be a non-anxious presence
to those around me,
a source of peace for those desperate for safety.

• • •

QUESTIONS TO PONDER

- What does a non-anxious presence look like in your life?
- How have anxious moments impacted how you operate in your day-to-day life?

Acknowledgments

A thousand thank-yous to the dream team at Brazos Press. You caught the vision for this devotional, and it's an honor to partner with you for a second time.

To my agent, Joy Reed: thank you for believing in my voice and writing. I'm forever grateful we found each other.

To the women who contributed to this book: you are all treasured voices, and I'm humbled to join forces with each of you.

To my fraternity (husband and sons): you all sacrificed a summer of beach days, berry picking, and paddleboarding so I could hole up in my office and churn out this title. Your collective support is not lost on me.

To those bearing intimate witness to my life: Jana, Melisa, Jamyrlyn, Lisa, Janna, Amanda, and Shoni, your combined support has meant so very much. More often than not, you've named what I couldn't see for myself. Thank you for your endless encouragement.

To the Bludds: we've grown up together, and your support reminds me of how beautiful it is to be deeply known by another. Thank you for your insights and musings, honest wrestlings and convictions.

To the Jensens: thank you for loving me so well for so long—twenty-five years. I'm convinced God is endlessly good and near to the brokenhearted because of your embodied witness. Watching my children light up as I did when they are with both of you reminds me how good it is to be loved by the likes of you.

To the Resisterhood: much of this work is inspired by our conversations. I'm endlessly thankful for the time we've spent stretching and growing together.

To the Sip community: walking with you month after month for the past nine years has been pure bliss. When I write, I often think of you all—your hopes, your losses, and your hunt for the beautiful. I pray this devotional draws you deeper into communion with the Divine and with each other.

To Prem Gideon: you took me off the streets when I was two days old, loved me as your own, and hoped to God I'd find the lifesaving knowledge of Jesus Christ for myself. Reconnecting with you to hear of my beginnings healed something in me on a cellular level. You, amma, are the woman I waited for.

Notes

Chapter 1 Holy and Whole

1. Tikva Frymer-Kensky, s.v. "Rahab: Bible," *Shalvi/Hyman Encyclopedia of Jewish Women*, Jewish Women's Archive, last updated June 23, 2021, https://jwa.org/encyclopedia/article/rahab-bible.

2. Kelly Main, "The $1.5 Trillion Self-Care Industry Has a Secret. Great Leaders Already Know İt," INC.com, March 9, 2023, https://www.inc.com/kelly-main/the-15-trillion-self-care-industry-has-a-secret-great-leaders-already-know-it.html.

3. Julia Lee, *Biting the Hand: Growing Up Asian in Black and White America* (New York: Henry Holt & Co, 2023), 201.

4. Pooja Lakshmin, *Real Self-Care: A Transformative Program for Redefining Wellness (Crystals, Cleanses, and Bubble Baths Not Included)* (New York: Penguin Life, 2023), xxv.

5. Lakshmin, *Real Self-Care*, 16.

Chapter 2 Last at the Cross

1. David Augsburger, "Silence, Patience, Presence," 2012 Baccalaureate Address, Fuller Seminary, *Fuller Studio*, https://fullerstudio.fuller.edu/silence-patience-presence/.

2. Cited in Augsburger, "Silence, Patience, Presence."

Chapter 3 Know Better, Do Better

1. "Jean Wiley," Digital SNCC Gateway, accessed February 23, 2024, https://snccdigital.org/people/jean-wiley.

2. "Oral History Interview with Jean Wiley," Civil Rights Movement Archive, October 26, 2001, https://www.crmvet.org/nars/wiley1 .htm. Emphasis is set as shown in the transcript.

3. "Oral History Interview with Jean Wiley."

Chapter 4 Mothers of the Movement

1. Brittany E. Wilson, "Pugnacious Precursors and the Bearer of Peace: Jael, Judith, and Mary in Luke 1:42," *Catholic Biblical Quarterly* 68, no. 3 (2006): 437–38.

2. Kelley Nikondeha, *The First Advent in Palestine: Reversals, Resistance, and the Ongoing Complexity of Hope* (Minneapolis: Broadleaf Books, 2022), 62.

Chapter 5 Dreams of the Matriarchs

1. Margot Lee Shetterly, "Katherine Johnson Biography," NASA, November 22, 2016, https://www.nasa.gov/centers-and-facilities /langley/katherine-johnson-biography/.

2. Catherine Clark Kroeger and Mary J. Evans, *The IVP Women's Bible Commentary* (Downers Grove, IL: InterVarsity, 2002), 609.

Chapter 6 Birthright

1. Brenda Bacon, "The Daughters of Zelophehad and the Struggle for Justice for Women," The Schechter Institute, December 7, 2003, https://schechter.edu/the-daughters-of-zelophehad-and-the -struggle-for-justice-for-women.

Chapter 7 Healing

1. This phrase alludes to the title of Bessel van der Kolk's bestseller, *The Body Keeps the Score: Brain, Mind, and Body in the Healing of Trauma* (New York: Penguin Books, 2014), which explores how the effects of trauma transform our brains and bodies.

2. K.J. Ramsey (@kjramseywrites), "If Scripture was sufficient to heal trauma, why did the Word become flesh + dwell among us?," Twitter, June 3, 2022, 12:51 p.m., https://twitter.com/kjramsey writes/status/1532812128305811456?s=20.

Chapter 8 Prayers of Our Mothers

1. Mark D. Roberts, "Thin Places: A Biblical Investigation," Patheos, accessed December 20, 2023, https://www.patheos.com /blogs/markdroberts/series/thin-places.

Chapter 9 Advocates for Rest

1. Walter Brueggemann, *Sabbath as Resistance: Saying No to the Culture of Now* (Louisville: Westminster John Knox, 2017), 5.

2. Phyllis Trible, "Bringing Miriam Out of the Shadows," *Bible Review* 5, no. 1 (February 1989): 14, https://www.baslibrary.org/bible-review/5/1/3.

3. Allan A. Boesak, "The Riverbank, the Seashore and the Wilderness: Miriam, Liberation and Prophetic Witness against Empire," *HTS Theological Studies* 73, no. 4 (2017): 1–15, http://www.scielo.org.za/scielo.php?script=sci_arttext&pid=S02599422201 7000400014.

4. Ruth Haley Barton, *Embracing Rhythms of Work and Rest: From Sabbath to Sabbatical and Back Again* (Downers Grove, IL: InterVarsity, 2022), 29.

5. Tricia Hersey, *Rest Is Resistance: A Manifesto* (Boston: Little, Brown, 2022), 62.

6. Tamar Meir, s.v. "Miriam: Midrash and Aggadah," *Shalvi/Hyman Encyclopedia of Jewish Women*, Jewish Women's Archive, accessed December 30, 2023, https://jwa.org/encyclopedia/article/miriam-midrash-and-aggadah.

Chapter 10 Lionhearted Liturgies

1. Charles Reagan Wilson, "Mississippi Rebels: Elvis Presley, Fannie Lou Hamer, and the South's Culture of Religious Music," *Southern Quarterly* 50, no. 2 (2013): 26.

2. Debra Michals, ed., "Fannie Lou Hamer," National Women's History Museum, 2017, www.womenshistory.org/education-resources/biographies/fannie-lou-hamer.

3. Bernice Johnson Reagon, "Let the Church Sing 'Freedom,'" *Black Music Research Journal* 7 (1987): 111.

4. Kay Mills, *This Little Light of Mine: The Life of Fannie Lou Hamer* (Lexington: University Press of Kentucky, 2007), 16.

5. Breanna K. Barber, "Tell It on the Mountain: Fannie Lou Hamer's Pastoral and Prophetic Styles of Leadership as Acts of Public Prayer" (undergraduate thesis, University of Montana, 2015), 1, https://scholarworks.umt.edu/cgi/viewcontent.cgi?article=1033&context=utpp.

6. Adelle M. Banks interview with Kate Clifford Larson, "Faith, Endurance of Civil Rights Activist Fannie Lou Hamer Revealed in New Biography," Religion News Service, October 5, 2021, https://religionnews.com/2021/10/05/faith-endurance-of-civil-rights-activist-fannie-lou-hamer-revealed-in-new-biography.

7. Kayla Craig, *To Light Their Way* (Carol Stream, IL: Tyndale, 2021), xxi.

Chapter 11 Get in Formation

1. Yazmine Nichols, "'Let's Get in Formation': Beyonce's Spiritual Call for Black Resistance," Religion Dispatches, February 19, 2016, https://religiondispatches.org/lets-get-in-formation-beyonces-spiritual-call-for-black-resistance.

Chapter 12 Crafting Conditions of Care

1. Kelley Nikondeha, *Defiant: What the Women of Exodus Teach Us about Freedom* (Grand Rapids: Eerdmans, 2020), 115.

2. Sally Roesch Wagner, "Haudenosaunee Influence on the Woman Suffrage Movement," Buffalo Toronto Public Media, accessed December 30, 2023, https://www.wned.org/television/wned-productions/wned-history-productions/discovering-new-york-suffrage-stories/haudenosaunee-influence-on-the-woman-suffrage-movement.

3. Wagner, "Haudenosaunee Influence."

Chapter 13 Lament to Heal

1. L. Juliana M. Claassens "Calling the Keeners: The Image of the Wailing Woman as Symbol of Survival in a Traumatized World," *Journal of Feminist Studies in Religion* 26, no. 1 (2010): 66, https://doi.org/10.2979/fsr.2010.26.1.63.

2. Claassens, "Calling the Keeners," 67–72.

3. Claassens, "Calling the Keeners," 67.

4. Jess Craig, "Violence in Cameroon's Anglophone Crisis Takes High Civilian Toll," Aljazeera, April 1, 2021, https://www.aljazeera.com/news/2021/4/1/violence-in-cameroon-anglophone-crisis-takes-high-civilian-toll.

5. "Cameroon," International Crisis Group, accessed December 30, 2023, https://www.crisisgroup.org/africa/central-africa/cameroon.

6. Gladys M. Ashu, "The Impact of the Anglophone Conflict on Women and Children and Their Advocacy for Peace in Cameroon," *Gender & Behaviour* 18, no. 1 (January 2020): 14829–844.

7. Ivoline Kefen Budji, "Utilizing Sounds of Mourning as Protest and Activism: The 2019 Northwestern Women's Lamentation March within the Anglophone Crisis in Cameroon," *Resonance: The Journal of Sound and Culture* 1, no. 4 (December 2020): 443–62, https://doi.org/10.1525/res.2020.1.4.443.

Chapter 14 A Culture of Belonging

1. "Septima Poinsette Clark: 1898–1987," Wander Women Project, accessed December 30, 2023, https://wanderwomenproject .com/women/septima-poinsette-clark.

2. Erin Blakemore, "The Woman Who Schooled the Civil Rights Movement" *Time*, February 16, 2016, https://time.com/4213751 /septima-clark-civil-rights-movement.

Chapter 15 Your Beautiful Body

1. Thanassis Samaras, "Aristotle on Gender in 'Politics' I," *History of Political Thought* 37, no. 4 (2016): 597, http://www.jstor .org/stable/26228720.

2. Tertullian, "On the Apparel of Women, Book 1," quoted in Mary Daly, *Beyond God the Father: Toward a Philosophy of Women's Liberation* (Boston: Beacon, 1973), 44.

3. "Racism and Rape," National Alliance to End Sexual Violence, accessed December 30, 2023, https://endsexualviolence.org /where_we_stand/racism-and-rape.

4. Philip B. Payne, "Examining the Twelve Biblical Pillars of Male Hierarchy," CBE International, October 31, 2012, https://www .cbeinternational.org/resource/article/examining-twelve-biblical -pillars-male-hierarchy.

5. Irenaeus, "Proof of the Apostolic Preachings," as quoted in Luigi Gambero, *Mary and the Fathers of the Church* (San Francisco: Ignatian Press, 1999), 55; see also Diliana N. Angelova, *Sacred Founders: Women, Men, and Gods in the Discourse of Imperial Founding, Rome through Early Byzantium* (Oakland: University of California Press, 2015), 242.

6. St. Ephraim, Diatessaron 2, quoted in Gambero, *Mary and the Fathers*, 117.

7. Hye Hyun Han, "The Eve and Mary Parallel: Misogyny in 1 Timothy 2:11–15," *Asian American Theological Forum* 9, no. 2 (May 2021): https://aatfweb.org/2021/05/28/the-eve-and-mary-paral lel-misogyny-in-1-timothy-211-15.

Chapter 16 Discernment

1. Henri Nouwen, *Discernment: Reading the Signs of Daily Life*, rev. ed. (New York: HarperCollins, 2015), 5.

2. Charles Spurgeon, quoted in Costi W. Hinn, *Knowing the Spirit* (Grand Rapids: Zondervan, 2023), 8. Hinn acknowledges that this attribution has proved difficult to verify.

Chapter 17 Gentleness

1. Judith Heumann and Kristen Joiner, *Being Heumann: An Unrepentant Memoir of a Disability Activist* (Boston: Beacon, 2020), 51.

2. Rebekah Taussig, "Judy Heumann Insisted Disabled People Like Me Belong," *Time*, March 8, 2023, https://time.com/6261131/judy-heumann-death-disability-essay.

3. As quoted in Joseph Shapiro, *No Pity: People with Disabilities Forging New Civil Rights Movement* (New York: Three Rivers Press, 1994), 20.

4. Jenny Palmiotto, "Wanna Judge Me?," Family Guidance and Therapy, December 14, 2018, https://familyguidanceandtherapy.com/the-circle-of-judgement-shame.

5. Judy Heumann, "Pulling Back the Curtain with Judy Heumann," *Ability*, December 2019, https://abilitymagazine.com/pulling-back-the-curtain/.

Chapter 18 Reclaiming What's Been Lost

1. This quotation comes from a blog post that preserves women's internment camp experiences, cited in Judi Cheng, "Japanese American Women in the Internment Camps," *Breaking the Chains*, February 14, 2022, https://www.breakingthechainsmag.org/japanese-american-women-in-the-internment-camps.

2. Nina Wallace, "Issei Mothers Played an Important—and Largely Forgotten—Role in the Japanese American Draft Resistance Movement," Denshō, May 5, 2021, https://densho.org/catalyst/issei-mothers-played-important-role-in-the-japanese-american-draft-resistance-movement.

3. Cheng, "Japanese American Women."

4. Lee B. Spitzer, "Embracing a Spiritual Discipline of Reparations," Word & Way, September 28, 2022, https://wordandway.org/2022/09/28/embracing-a-spiritual-discipline-of-reparations.

5. Duke L. Kwon and Gregory Thompson, *Reparations: A Christian Call for Repentance and Repair* (Grand Rapids: Brazos, 2021), 178.

Chapter 19 Befriending Grief

1. "Who Was Ella Baker?," Ella Baker Center for Human Rights, accessed December 30, 2023, https://ellabakercenter.org/who-was-ella-baker.

2. Stephen Preskill, "Fundi: The Enduring Leadership Legacy of Civil Rights Activist Ella Baker," *Advancing Women in Leadership*

Journal 18 (Spring 2005), https://awl-ojs-tamu.tdl.org/awl/article/view/476.

3. Preskill, "Fundi."

4. Francis Weller, *The Wild Edge of Sorrow: Rituals of Renewal and the Sacred Work of Grief* (Berkeley: North Atlantic Books, 2015), 10.

Chapter 20 Her Story

1. Tamar Kadari, s.v. "Vashti: Midrash and Aggadah," *Shalvi/Hyman Encyclopedia of Jewish Women*, Jewish Women's Archive, December 31, 1991, https://jwa.org/encyclopedia/article/vashti-midrash-and-aggadah.

2. Annette Griffin, "Was Vashti Really in the Wrong in Esther's Story?," Bible Study Tools, September 10, 2021, https://www.biblestudytools.com/bible-study/topical-studies/was-vashti-really-in-the-wrong-in-esthers-story.html.

3. Timothy K. Beal, *Book of Hiding: Gender, Ethnicity, Annihilation, and Esther* (New York: Routledge, 1997), 22.

4. Yvonne Sherwood, *The Bible and Feminism: Remapping the Field* (New York: Oxford University Press, 2017), 349.

Chapter 21 The Stories We Tell Ourselves

1. God's promise to Abram and Sarai's subsequent handing over of her servant Hagar are found in Genesis 15–16.

2. Viola Davis, *Finding Me: A Memoir* (New York: HarperCollins, 2023), 18.

3. Anne Lamott, *Almost Everything: Notes on Hope* (New York: Penguin, 2018), 94 (emphasis added).

Chapter 22 Waiting

1. Elisabeth Elliot, *Passion and Purity: Learning to Bring Your Love Life Under Christ's Control* (Grand Rapids: Revell, 2002), 61–62.

Chapter 24 Despair and the Divine

1. Mary Elizabeth Baxter, "Hagar," Blue Letter Bible, accessed December 30, 2023, https://www.blueletterbible.org/Comm/baxter_mary/WitW/WitW05_Hagar.cfm.

2. Ekemini Uwan, Christina Edmondson, and Michelle Higgins, *Truth's Table: Black Women's Musings on Life, Love, and Liberation* (New York: Crown, 2022), 267.

3. Ron Rolheiser, OMI, "When Feeling Down and Out," August 21, 2005, https://ronrolheiser.com/when-feeling-down-and-out.

Chapter 25 Collateral Damage

1. Al Chukwuma Okoli, "Gender and Terror: Boko Harem and the Abuse of Women in Nigeria," *Georgetown Journal of International Affairs*, April 5, 2022, https://gjia.georgetown.edu/2022/04/05/gender-and-terror-boko-haram-and-the-abuse-of-women-in-nigeria.

2. The Hebrew allows for either a personal or an impersonal pronoun.

3. Kathleen Parker, "Women Aren't Pet Rocks," *Washington Post*, April 1, 2011, https://www.washingtonpost.com/opinions/women-arent-pet-rocks/2011/04/01/AFTU4wJC_story.html.

Chapter 27 Magnificent Refuge

1. Modern interpreters suggest she struggled with ecstatic epilepsy due to a lesion in her temporal lobe.

2. Kieran Kavanaugh, ed., *St. Teresa of Avila: The Way of Perfection* (Washington, DC: ICS Publications, 2000), 23.

3. Teresa of Ávila, *The Interior Castle* (New York: Penguin, 2004), introduction.

4. Thomas Merton, *Contemplative Prayer* (New York: Crown, 2009), 4.

5. Teresa of Ávila, *Interior Castle*, 194.

Chapter 28 Navigating Burnout

1. Alfreda M. Duster, "Introduction," in Ida B. Wells, *Crusade for Justice: The Autobiography of Ida B. Wells*, ed. Alfreda M. Duster (Chicago: University of Chicago Press, 1970), xiv.

2. Duster, "Introduction," xxxi.

3. Duster, "Introduction," xiv.

4. Duster, "Introduction," xvii. Diary entry of Ida B. Wells for April 11, 1887 (unpublished).

5. Wells, *Crusade for Justice*, 414.

6. Noman B. Wood, *The White Side of a Black Subject* (Chicago: American Publishing House, 1897), 381–82.

Chapter 29 Righteous Defiance

1. David Daube, *Civil Disobedience in Antiquity* (Eugene, OR: Wipf & Stock, 2011), 5.

2. Al-Monitor Staff, "Iran Says Average Age of Protestors Is 15," Al-Monitor, October 5, 2022, https://www.al-monitor.com/originals /2022/10/iran-says-average-age-arrested-protesters-15.

3. Sanya Mansoor, "How Iran's Morality Police Enforces a Strict Interpretation of Islamic Law," *Time*, November 10, 2022, https:// time.com/6230535/iran-morality-police-mahsa-amini-hijab.

4. "From Protest Symbol to State Imposition: The Story of Hijab in Iran," Outlook India, April 12, 2023, https://www.outlookindia .com/international/from-protest-symbol-to-state-imposition-the -story-of-hijab-in-iran-photos-277843.

5. Imam Hariri-Kia, "The Morality Police and Me," The Cut, December 15, 2022, https://www.thecut.com/2022/12/my-encoun ters-with-irans-morality-police.html.

6. Kelley Nikondeha, *Defiant: What the Women of Exodus Teach Us about Freedom* (Grand Rapids: Eerdmans, 2020), 40.

Chapter 30 Steadfast Joy

1. Hebrew Lexicon, Bible Study Tools, https://www.biblestudy tools.com/lexicons/hebrew/nas/maowz.html.

2. Charlotte M. Kelly, "A Saintly Savage: Kateri Takakwitha." *The Irish Monthly* 63, no. 746 (1935): 531, http://www.jstor.org/stable /20513797.

3. "Our Patron Saint: St. Kateri Tekakwitha," Saint Kateri Conservation Center, accessed February 10, 2024, https://www.kateri .org/our-patron-saint/.

4. "Our Patron Saint."

5. This quotation is attributed to Barbara Brown Taylor by Joe Albright, "Overwhelmed with Joy," Dial Hope, December 31, 2021, https://www.dialhope.org/overwhelmed-with-joy.

Chapter 31 Carry One Another

1. Pascal Mannaerts, "The Widows Who Can't Return Home," BBC, February 24, 2022, https://www.bbc.com/travel/article/20160 907-the-widows-who-cant-return-home.

2. Jean Chapman, "Violence against Women in Democratic India: Let's Talk Misogyny," *Social Scientist* 42, nos. 9–10 (2014): 56, http://www.jstor.org/stable/24372976.

3. Kai Schultz, "India's Widows, Abused at Home, Have Sought Refuge in This Holy City for Centuries," *New York Times*, August 27, 2019, https://www.nytimes.com/2019/08/27/world/asia/india -women-widows.html.

4. Chapman, "Violence against Women," 56.

5. Schultz, "India's Widows."

6. Chapman, "Violence against Women," 57.

7. Schultz, "India's Widows."

8. Brené Brown, *Braving the Wilderness: The Quest for True Belonging and the Courage to Stand Alone* (New York: Random House, 2017), 120.

9. W. James Booth, *Communities of Memory: On Witness, Identity, and Justice* (Ithaca, NY: Cornell University Press, 2006), 112–63.

10. Maya Angelou, *I Know Why the Caged Bird Sings*, 2nd ed. (New York: Random House, 2010), 74.

Chapter 32 Bearing Witness

1. This insight from D. T. Niles is referenced in Mark Woods, "Why Did Jesus Really Ask the Samaritan Woman for a Drink?," *Christian Today*, May 16, 2017, https://www.christiantoday.com /article/why-did-jesus-really-ask-the-samaritan-woman-for-a-drink /109229.htm.

2. Craig S. Farmer, "Changing Images of the Samaritan Woman in Early Reformed Commentaries on John," *Church History* 65, no. 3 (1996): 366.

3. David Guznik, "John 4: A Samaritan Woman and a Nobleman Meet Jesus," Enduring Word, accessed December 30, 2023, https://enduringword.com/bible-commentary/john-4.

4. Rose Mukansengimana-Nyirimana and Jonathan A. Draper, "The Peacemaking Role of the Samaritan Woman in John 4:1–42: A Mirror and Challenge to Rwandan Women," *Neotestamentica* 46, no. 2 (2012): 299–318.

5. Farmer, "Changing Images of the Samaritan Woman," 365.

Chapter 33 Arrival

1. Sondra A. O'Neale, "Phillis Wheatley (1753–84)," Poetry Foundation, https://www.poetryfoundation.org/poets/phillis-wheatley.

2. J. Luebering, s.v. "Phillis Wheatley," *Encyclopedia Britannica*, January 27, 2023, https://www.britannica.com/biography/Phillis -Wheatley.

3. Patricia C. Willis, "Phillis Wheatley, George Whitefield, and the Countess of Huntingdon in the Beinecke Library," *Yale University Library Gazette* 80, no. 3/4 (2006): 164, http://www.jstor.org/stable/4085 9549.

4. Phillis Wheatley, "On Being Brought from Africa to America," Poetry Foundation, https://www.poetryfoundation.org/poems /45465/on-being-brought-from-africa-to-america.

5. "St. Theresa's Prayer," Sisters of the Divine Savior, accessed December 30, 2023, https://www.sistersofthedivinesavior.org/pray_archive/st-theresas-prayer.

Chapter 34 We Go High

1. Tamar Kadari, s.v. "Huldah, the Prophet: Midrash and Aggadah," *Shalvi/Hyman Encyclopedia of Jewish Women*, Jewish Women's Archive, December 31, 1999, https://jwa.org/encyclopedia/article/huldah-prophet-midrash-and-aggadah.

2. Abraham Kuyper, *Women of the Old Testament*, trans. Henry Zylstra (Grand Rapids: Zondervan, 1961), 106.

3. Raisa Bruner, "Michelle Obama Explains What Going High Really Means," *Time*, November 20, 2018, https://time.com/5459984/michelle-obama-go-high.

Chapter 36 Consent to Reality

1. "About Immaculée," accessed December 30, 2023, https://www.immaculee.com/pages/about.

2. "About Immaculée."

3. Immaculée Ilibagiza, with Steve Erwin, *Left to Tell: Discovering God amidst the Rwandan Holocaust* (New York: Hay House, 2007), 197.

4. Layli Maparyan, *The Womanist Idea* (New York: Routledge, 2012), 196.

5. Christiana Ibilola Awosan, interview with Erica Sloan, "How to Let Go of Lingering Resentment and Achieve Peace of Mind, According to Mental Health Experts," Well + Good, November 22, 2021, https://www.wellandgood.com/how-to-let-go-of-resentment.

6. S. Davidai and T. Gilovich, "The Ideal Road Not Taken: The Self-Discrepancies Involved in People's Most Enduring Regrets," *Emotion* 18, no. 3 (2018): 439–52.

7. Henri J. M. Nouwen, *The Return of the Prodigal Son: A Story of Homecoming*, rev. ed. (Colorado Springs: Convergent, 2016), 84.

8. Anne Gene Broomhall, Wendy J. Phillips, Donald W. Hine, and Natasha M. Loi, "Upward Counterfactual Thinking and Depression: A Meta-Analysis, *Clinical Psychology Review* 55 (2017): 56–73.

Chapter 37 Hospitality amid Hostility

1. Diane Pien, "Black Panther Party's Free Breakfast Program (1969–1980)," Black Past, February 11, 2010, https://www.blackpast.org/african-american-history/black-panther-partys-free-breakfast-program-1969-1980.

2. Pien, "Black Panther Party's Free Breakfast Program."

3. Pien, "Black Panther Party's Free Breakfast Program."

4. "School Meal Statistics," School Nutrition Association, accessed December 30, 2023, https://schoolnutrition.org/about-school-meals/school-meal-statistics.

5. Nik Heynen, "Bending the Bars of Empire from Every Ghetto for Survival: The Black Panther Party's Radical Antihunger Politics of Social Reproduction and Scale," *Annals of the Association of American Geographers* 99, no. 2 (2009): 406–22, doi.org/10.1080/00045600802683767.

6. David Hackett Fisher, *Liberty and Freedom: A Visual History of America's Founding Ideas* (New York: Oxford University Press, 2004), 5.

7. Cole Arthur Riley, *This Here Flesh: Spirituality, Liberation, and the Stories That Make Us* (New York: Crown, 2022), 77.

Chapter 38 Who Are We Becoming?

1. Angela Davis, *Women, Culture, and Politics* (New York: Vintage, 1990), 129.

2. Sara Farris, *In the Name of Women's Rights: The Rise of Femonationalism* (Durham, NC: Duke University Press, 2017).

3. Chimamanda Ngozi Adichie, "The Danger of a Single Story," TEDglobal, July 2009, https://www.ted.com /talks/chimamanda_ngozi_adichie_the_danger_of_a_single_story?language=en.

Chapter 39 Love Is the Final Fight

1. Donald Davidson, as quoted in Herbert Lockyer, *All the Women of the Bible* (Grand Rapids: Zondervan, 1967), 143.

2. Wilda Gafney, *Womanist Midrash: A Reintroduction to the Women of the Torah and the Throne* (Louisville: Westminster John Knox, 2017), 201.

3. John Perkins, *Dream with Me: Race, Love, and the Struggle We Must Win* (Grand Rapids: Baker Books, 2017), 30.

4. Cornel West, *Living and Loving Out Loud: A Memoir* (Carlsbad, CA: Hay House, 2009), 232.

Chapter 40 Becoming a Non-anxious Presence

1. Ummekulsoom Shekhani, "Sarojini Naidu: The Forgotten Orator of India," *Rhetoric Review* 36, no. 2 (April 2017): 139–50.

2. Sita Anantha Raman, s.v. "Naidu, Sarojini," *Encyclopedia of India*, ed. Stanley Wolpert (New York: Scribner's Sons, 2006), 3:212–13.

3. The word *satyagraha* comes from Hindi and Sanskit origins and means "holding on to truth." Gandhi used the term to refer to nonviolent civil resistance.

4. Kenneth Pletcher, s.v. "Salt March," *Encyclopedia Britannica*, last updated January 5, 2024, https://www.britannica.com /event/Salt-March.

5. Raman, "Naidu, Sarojini," 3:212–13.

6. Sarojini Naidu, *The Golden Threshold* (1905; repr., London: William Heinemann, 2006), 49.

7. "From Syria to the Olympics: A Tale of Two Sisters Swimming for Their Lives," IOM UN Blog, accessed December 30, 2023, https://weblog.iom.int/syria-olympics-tale-two-sisters-swimming -their-lives.

8. Edwin H. Friedman, *Generation to Generation: Family Process in Church and Synagogue* (New York: Guilford, 2011), 8.

TIFFANY BLUHM is the author of *Prey Tell: Why We Silence Women Who Tell the Truth and How Everyone Can Speak Up* as well as *She Dreams* and *Never Alone* and their companion Bible studies. With over fifteen years of experience in ministry and nonprofit leadership, she speaks, writes, and leads at the intersection of justice and faith for conferences, churches, and colleges. Her work has been featured in *Publishers Weekly*, the YouVersion Bible app, *Sojourners*, *Propel Ecclesia*, and more. She lives in the Pacific Northwest with her husband and two sons.

Connect with Tiffany:

www.tiffanybluhm.com

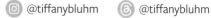

TiffanyABluhm   @tiffanybluhm

@tiffanybluhm   @tiffanybluhm